Great War Literature

NOTES

Written by W Lawrance

on

All Quiet on the Western Front

A Novel by Erich Maria Remarque

Great War Literature Notes on All Quiet on the Western Front, a novel by Erich Maria Remarque
Written by W Lawrance

Published by:
Great War Literature Publishing LLP
Forum House, Stirling Road, Chichester, PO19 7DN
Web site: *www.greatwarliterature.co.uk*
E-Mail: *admin@greatwarliterature.co.uk*

Produced in Great Britain

First Published 2006.
This Edition published 2014. Copyright ©2005-2014 Wendy Lawrance.
The moral right of the author has been asserted.

ISBN 978-1910603079 Paperback Edition 2
Replaces earlier edition: 978-1905378302

10 9 8 7 6 5 4 3 2 1

All rights reserved: no part of this publication may be reproduced, stored in a retrieval system, or transmitted in any form or by any means, electronic, mechanical, photocopying or otherwise, without the prior written consent of Great War Literature Publishing LLP.

Great War Literature Publishing LLP reserve the right to amend this document without any prior notification.

This study guide is sold subject to the condition that it shall not, by way of trade or otherwise, be lent, re-sold, hired out or otherwise circulated without the publisher's prior consent in any form of binding or cover other than that in which it is published and without similar conditions being imposed on the subsequent purchaser.

Design and production by Great War Literature Publishing LLP
Typeset in Neue Helvetica, ITC Berkeley Old Style and Trajan Pro

Great War Literature Notes on

All Quiet on the Western Front

CONTENTS

Preface	5
Introduction	7
Synopsis	9
Character Analysis	31
Paul Bäumer	31
Stanislaus Katczinsky	36
Albert Kropp	38
Corporal Himmelstoss	40
Kantorek	41
Themes	43
Waste and Futility	43
Comradeship	45
Complacency at Home	47
Horror of War	49
Comparisons	51
Male Relationships	51
Home Front	54
Waste and Futility	58
Language	60
Characters	62
Biography of Erich Maria Remarque	65
Further Reading Recommendations	69
Bibliography	77
Other Titles	79

Preface

The primary purpose of Great War Literature Study Guides is to provide in-depth analysis of First World War literature for GCSE and A-Level students.

Great War Literature Publishing have taken the positive decision to produce a uniquely detailed and in-depth interpretation of selected works for students. We also actively promote the publication of our works in an electronic format via the Internet to give the broadest possible access.

Our publications can be used in isolation or in collaboration with other study guides. It is our aim to provide assistance with your understanding of First World War literature, not to provide the answers to specific questions. This approach provides the resources that allow the student the freedom to reach their own conclusions and express an independent viewpoint.

The structure of Great War Literature Study Guides allows the reader to delve into a required section easily without the need to read from beginning to end.

The Great War Literature Study Guides have been thoroughly researched and are the result of over 30 years of experience of studying this particular genre.

Studying literature is not about being right or wrong, it is entirely a matter of opinion. The secret to success is developing the ability to form these opinions and to deliver them succinctly and reinforce them with quotes and clear references from the text.

Great War Literature Study Guides help to extend your knowledge of First World War literature and offer clear definitions and guidance to enhance your studying. Our clear and simple layouts make the guides easy to access and understand.

The Great War Literature Study Guide on *All Quiet on the Western Front*, provides a critical assessment of many aspects of this novel and is based entirely on the opinion of the author of this guide.

Introduction

All Quiet on the Western Front, which was published in 1929, is probably the most realistic anti-war novel written on the subject of the First World War. Its author's first-hand experience of life in the German trenches gives this novel an authenticity, which is somehow lacking in much of what has been written since.

Remarque's overriding theme throughout the story is the waste of life and loss of youth, innocence, hope and ambition caused by his characters' experiences in the trenches. His use of graphic, uncompromising language reinforces the horror of the First World War, leaving little or nothing to the reader's imagination.

This is an invaluable book to both students and those with a particular interest in this genre for many reasons. These include the fact that it was written by someone who was actually there; that it was written from a German perspective and also that, unlike most literature from the First World War, its characters are mainly from the ranks, rather than being officers. This makes *All Quiet on the Western Front* particularly useful to those who are making comparisons between different forms of First World War literature.

This novel breaks the war down into a human experience, involving all sorts of activities from learning how to kill a man with a spade, to the discovery that, not far behind the lines, butterflies still roam above flower-filled meadows. Ultimately, however, it is the de-humanising effects of the war which come to dominate: summed up by the realisation of a very young man that all of his friends are dead, and that his life no longer has any meaning or purpose; that everything, for which he had been lead to believe he was fighting, has already gone, because he has no future to return home to. This is not a book about right and wrong, or friend and foe - it shows us that all of the men have everything to live for, none of them want to die, none of them want a war and, above all, the suffering is universal.

W Lawrance
November 2014

ALL QUIET ON THE WESTERN FRONT
BY ERICH MARIA REMARQUE

SYNOPSIS

CHAPTER 1

The novel opens behind the lines, where a group of men, recently returned from the trenches have just enjoyed a hearty meal. They are relieved and restful, but as there is extra food to spare, some of them stock up for later. The men also receive extra cigarettes, which they really appreciate. The reason for the surplus food and tobacco is that the quartermaster, who is responsible for supplying the troops, had ordered enough supplies for 150 men. However, after two weeks in the front line, only 80 men have returned. Paul Bäumer, the narrator of the story, introduces the reader to his comrades: Kropp, Müller, and Leer had all been in Paul's class at school and had enlisted together. Their new friends are Tjaden, Westhus, Detering and Katczinsky, who is also called Kat.

Paul recalls that the cook had, at first, refused to serve them until *all* the men were present. He had believed that there were more men to follow and did not want those who were there to take everything, leaving nothing for whoever came last. However, when he had learned that so many men had died, he had been quite put out, and had wanted to keep back the extra portions. He had maintained this stance, until he had been instructed by the company commander to dish out all of the food, rather than waste almost half of it. This had given the men great satisfaction, particularly Tjaden, who had become angry at the cook's grudging attitude.

The next day, the mail arrives, so the men are happy. They go for a walk behind the billets, where they discover three wooden boxes which will make excellent toilets. They form a circle and sit for a couple of hours. Paul remembers how, as raw recruits, the use of open latrines had proved a great source of embarrassment. Now, however, he and his friends take such matters in their stride. As they sit on these home-made toilets, they play cards, read their mail and smoke. They also discuss another comrade, from their schooldays, Kemmerich, who has been wounded in the thigh and is in hospital. They decide that they will go and visit their friend later that day. Albert Kropp has received a letter from Kantorek, their old schoolmaster and Paul remembers how Kantorek had bullied them all into enlisting. He recalls another class-mate, Joseph Behm, who had been more reluctant than the rest, but had gone along with everyone else, so as not to be left out. Behm had received a wound in the eye and been knocked unconscious. Upon waking, he had wandered, blindly, about No Man's Land and had been shot. Paul feels that he and his friends have learned a harsh lesson - to trust only in each other.

On the assumption that Kemmerich will soon be going home, the men pack up his belongings and take them to the hospital. When they arrive, however, it immediately becomes clear that Kemmerich will not be going anywhere: his leg has been amputated and his comrades recognise in his face the signs of his impending death. Despite unhappy memories of parting from their families and the way that Kemmerich's distraught mother had begged Paul to take care of her son, the friends do their best to cheer their dying comrade. He does not understand the severity of his wounds and they discuss him going home. Müller discovers Kemmerich's boots under the bed - they are an English airman's boots, made of leather, so he asks Kemmerich if he may keep them. Kemmerich, unaware that he will have no further use for them, refuses. The friends take their leave and Paul promises to visit again the next day. Kropp is angry that their friend is going to die and violently instructs an orderly to give Kemmerich some morphia. On the way back to their billets, they reflect on their lost youth.

CHAPTER 2

Paul continues to think about the effect which the war is having on his generation: they were too young to have experienced very much of life before the war, but afterwards, they will not know how to pick up the threads of their lives, because, despite their youth, they are no longer 'young'. He also ponders how the army has managed to change them all so much in such a short space of time. Paul remembers the harsh training under the watchful eye of Corporal Himmelstoss. This man seemed to delight in the suffering of his recruits. Eventually, his tortures had got the better of the men and Kropp and Paul had 'accidentally' tipped a bucket full of excrement over the furious corporal. His threats to report them carried no weight, however, as Kropp had countered this with his own threat: to reveal the harsh nature of their treatment under Himmelstoss. The corporal had been so deflated by this threat that he had seemed to lose his hold over the men. Now that Paul is more experienced, he can appreciate the value of his training: it has prepared him for the horror of the trenches and made them all realise the value of their friendship.

The next day, Paul visits Kemmerich again. His deterioration has continued and he now knows about his leg. This knowledge has resulted in him giving up hope. He tells Paul to take his boots and give them to Müller. Paul stays with him and tries to rally his spirits - talking of a convalescent home and the improvements in artificial limbs, while the orderlies hover, impatient for the bed to become available. Paul notices that Kemmerich is quietly weeping and can think of nothing more to say to his old friend. Suddenly Kemmerich becomes much worse and Paul rushes out to find help. The doctor refuses to follow, but an orderly accompanies Paul back to Kemmerich's bedside, where they find him dead. The orderly wants the bed cleared immediately, so Paul removes Kemmerich's belongings and leaves. He runs back to his billet, rejoicing that he is still alive. When he arrives, he gives the boots to Müller.

CHAPTER 3

New recruits arrive, making Paul and his friends feel like aging veterans. Kat has managed to scrounge some cold meat and beans, some of which he offers to one of the recruits, pointing out, quite kindly, that in future, the recruit should bring something by way of payment for food. Naturally, he says to his friends, he does not expect payment from them. Paul reflects on the value of having a friend like Kat, who manages to find straw for bedding, food and cooking equipment, where others believe there is nothing to be had.

The men are now settled into their billets and they have time for debate and discussion. Kropp believes that the war could have been settled by a more fair and democratic means if the leaders of all the countries had fought it out amongst themselves. The men reminisce about their days in the barracks, which seem palatial compared to their current situation. They wonder whether Corporal Himmelstoss can have always been so mean, and Kat concludes that, like many officers, a little power has gone to his head. As they reflect on this idea, an excited Tjaden appears, bearing news: Himmelstoss has been sent to the front.

Tjaden, we learn, is especially bitter towards Himmelstoss. This stems from an event which had taken place at the barracks. It would seem that Tjaden had a problem with bed-wetting, which had quickly come to the attention of Himmelstoss, whose idea for 'curing' this problem was to find another man with the same problem, and place them in the same bunk beds, one above the other. Each night, one man would urinate over the other; the next night their positions would be altered, so the other man would get a soaking. Joined by Westhus, the men remember their joy at finally getting their revenge on Himmelstoss. They had ambushed him on a dark night, wrapped him in a bedspread and beaten him.

CHAPTER 4

Paul's company has been ordered to the front line to lay barbed wire. They travel in lorries, under the cover of darkness and, as they approach the front lines, Paul and Kat both hear some geese cackling. Kat remarks that he will return later to collect this potential meal.

When they reach the artillery lines, to the rear of the trenches, the guns are already firing. The new recruits are nervous, but the old-hands merely point out that something must be amiss, as the English have started firing an hour ahead of their usual time. Kat predicts that there will be heavy gunfire.

Paul reflects how, at the front, he feels that man and the earth have a closer bond than anywhere else. The lorries depart - they will return before dawn to take the men back to their billets. Paul and his company go up to the front line and when they arrive, Kat's predicted bombardment begins. The men perform their dangerous task with plenty of time to spare, so some of them try to sleep until the lorries return. Although they are behind the front lines, some of the bombs land nearby and the recruits begin to panic. A young soldier is so terrified that he crawls up to Paul and nestles in his arms. When the barrage lifts, it becomes clear that the young boy has emptied his bowels into his underpants. He is embarrassed, but Paul is sympathetic and tells him to go behind a nearby bush and discard his soiled underwear.

The men become aware of the cries of some wounded horses. Deterring, as a farmer, is particularly disturbed by this and cries out for someone to shoot the horses. Müller has some binoculars and they are able to make out the wounded animals, running around in terror. Deterring wants to shoot the horses himself, but Kat stops him: he cannot see the animals well enough to be sure that he would hit them. Eventually some stretcher-bearers, who are nearer the scene, shoot and kill the wounded animals. Deterring is angry that horses are used in the war.

At three o'clock in the morning, the men begin their journey back to meet the lorries. As they approach a cemetery the barrage suddenly flares up again. They take cover in the graveyard as the shells fall all around them. Paul is hit by splinters of wood from the coffins which are being unearthed by the bombardment. He shelters under a coffin, before lunging towards a nearby shell-hole where he finds Kat, who seems to be shouting something inaudible. In a briefly quiet moment, Paul understands what it is that Kat is trying to say - 'Gas!' As he pulls on his own gas-mask, Paul notices one of the recruits who seems unaware of the alarm, and helps him with his mask. These two, Kat and

Kropp shelter in the shell-hole. A coffin lands on the recruit, injuring his arm. Kropp stops the wounded man from removing his gas-mask in his panic, while Paul and Kat free the man's arm and bandage it. As the bombardment ceases it becomes clear that they may safely remove their gas-masks and they help the wounded man out of the shell-hole. They come across another wounded recruit and Kropp goes on ahead with the man who had injured his arm while Paul and Kat tend to this recruit, who has a bad injury to his hip. As they cut open his trousers, they find that he is not wearing underpants and Paul realises that this is the young man who had been so frightened earlier. His wounds are so severe that Kat thinks it would be kinder to shoot him, rather than allow him to die in pain, as they are sure he will. Before they can act, however, stretcher-bearers arrive and the recruit is removed, with the other wounded. The men return to find the lorries and are taken back to their billets.

CHAPTER 5

The men sit in the warm sunshine, removing lice from their shirts and talking. They are preoccupied with the arrival of Himmelstoss, who it would seem has been transferred to the front because he was being too rough with the recruits. Müller asks everyone, in turn, what they would do if the war suddenly ended. Kropp says he would get drunk; Kat shows them a photograph of his wife and curses the war; Haie Westhus announces that he would jump into bed with the first woman he came across, but then reveals that he would stay in the army, serve out his twelve years and then become a policeman. Tjaden, on the other hand, is only concerned with getting his revenge on Himmelstoss. Deterring says that he would return to his farm.

The men notice Himmelstoss approaching and he waits by the group, expecting them to stand to attention in his presence. The men, particularly Tjaden, are openly antagonistic and although Himmelstoss tries to exert his authority, he gets nowhere and storms off to report Tjaden's insubordination. The others are worried that their friend will be punished, but Tjaden seems to feel that insulting Himmelstoss was worth it. He, Westhus and Leer make themselves scarce before Himmelstoss can return.

The remaining men discuss their old schoolmaster, Kantorek and the number of their classmates who have been killed or wounded. Paul reflects that nothing they were taught at school has done them any good at the front. They realise how lost they feel: the older men have lives to return to, but the young will have to begin again.

Himmelstoss returns with a sergeant-major, but they fail to find Tjaden and demand that he be found and report to them in ten minutes. Tjaden decides to ignore this order and when Himmelstoss returns, Kropp lashes out at the corporal. That evening, a trial is held before Lieutenant Bertinck. Paul reveals the reason behind Tjaden's bitterness towards Himmelstoss. Bertinck is angry with Himmelstoss and although he punishes Tjaden and Kropp, he is as lenient as he can be.

Later that night, Paul and Kat go back to the place where they heard the geese. After a difficult altercation with a dog, Paul manages to secure one goose and the two men find a hut in which to roast it. As it cooks, Paul dozes and reflects on his friendship with Kat - who he holds in great esteem. They eat some of the goose, once it is ready and agree to take the rest to Kropp and Tjaden, who are still under open arrest.

CHAPTER 6

Amid rumours of an attack, the men return to the front earlier than expected. En-route, they pass a ruined school-house beside which lie dozens of newly-built pine coffins. They try to see the humourous side of this ominous sight, but deep-down, they know this means they are in for a tough time. They can sense that the English have brought up new artillery, but the first shells to land near them are German: their guns are so worn that they no longer fire accurately.

Paul ponders on the element of luck. He has had previous narrow escapes from death and knows that, like all soldiers, he owes his survival to chance more than anything else. The dugout is plagued by rats, who eagerly consume the men's bread ration. The soldiers invent different ways of preventing this and killing the rats. A ration of cheese and rum is given out, which makes the men suspicious that they are due for a particularly bad time. During the day, they keep busy, removing saw edges from bayonets because such weapons are guaranteed to anger the enemy, who react violently towards anyone they catch carrying a saw-edged bayonet. Paul reflects, however, that a spade is a more valuable weapon than a bayonet anyway.

At night there are gas attacks and the men nervously anticipate the expected hostilities. As the days pass, the men become more and more tired and anxious; rumours abound, but still nothing happens. Then one night, while the men are in the dugout, a huge bombardment begins. Bombs fall all around and in the morning, men stagger in from the observation posts, their nerves shattered. Panic begins to spread, especially among the new recruits, as the bombardment continues. At one stage the men are buried and must dig themselves out. In addition, they are hungry and thirsty, as the bombardment has made it impossible to bring up food and supplies. Even Kat fails to scrounge any food and the men become desperate, eating scraps of old bread.

Eventually, one of the recruits is overcome with panic and tries to escape from the dugout. Paul and Kat stop him, forcefully: they know that they must quell this panic before it spreads to the other men. After another particularly heavy barrage, three more recruits panic and try to flee; one succeeds and before Paul can go after him, he is bowled over by another blast. When Paul recovers, he sees that the recruit has been blown to pieces. The men try to keep themselves occupied by playing cards, but there is too much tension for them to concentrate and they grow weaker.

All at once they realise that the barrage has lifted and that they are under attack. From somewhere, the men find an inner strength and although they are initially forced to retreat, they manage to repulse the attack. This is a vicious battle and Paul often feels like giving up, but continues to fight ferociously in order to preserve his own life, just as his opponents do. He feels as though he is possessed by an unknown force which drives him on, regardless of the horrendous sights which surround him. Eventually, the fighting ceases and the men fall back to their own front line again, but they grab some food from the enemy dugouts before departing.

As evening approaches, the men, now back in their own trenches again, are exhausted, but continue with their duties. Paul is on sentry duty and tries, in the misty darkness, to gather his thoughts - a difficult process for a man who feels that he has lost his past and cannot see any hope for his future. When he is relieved from his duty, he goes back to the dugout and has some food. The other men seem more relaxed because the bombardment has stopped, but Paul remains thoughtful.

As the days pass, there are further attacks and the bodies begin to mount up in No Man's Land. Many of the wounded are rescued but some are stranded and the men have to listen to their cries for help. One particular victim causes great distress and they search for him for two days, hearing him continually crying out for help. They are unable to find him and eventually he falls silent and they know that he has died. His body will now swell and rot with all the others and add to the nauseating stench that drifts across No Man's Land.

At night the men venture out to collect parts of the French star shells which have landed in No Man's Land, for which they have various uses. Now that the trench is quieter, Paul has time to notice that nature continues as before - butterflies and birds still fly about, and at least the rats no longer trouble them because they are feeding on the corpses which continue to pile up due to the accuracy of the enemy shelling, which is not unduly heavy but, thanks to the observation planes, seems to always hit its target.

As the bombardment increases again, new recruits arrive to join in the defence of the sector. They are of little use, however, as their inexperience usually results in an early death. Although only 20 himself, Paul is struck by how young these recruits are - to him they seem like children.

One day, during the shelling, Paul and Himmelstoss seek shelter in the same dugout, along with several other men. When they all get up to go back out into the trench, anticipating an attack, Paul notices that Himmelstoss is not among them. He returns to the dugout and finds Himmelstoss cowering, pretending to be injured. Paul is furious and orders his former tormentor into the trenches.

Despite his attempts to physically force Himmelstoss outside, they remain there until a lieutenant orders them to join the others. Himmelstoss obeys this order as though he had not even been aware of Paul's presence.

This scenario of bombardments, attacks and counter-attacks continues for days and the men become exhausted. In moments of rest, they train the new recruits, giving these boys the benefit of their experience. It is to no avail, however, as whenever there is an attack, the youngsters panic and forget everything they have been taught. Haie Westhus is fatally wounded in his back and is taken away on a stretcher, knowing that he will die. The sights which
Paul witnesses and the horrors that surround him are nauseating and distressing, yet they manage to hold their ground despite enormous losses.

Eventually, when they are relieved, the remains of Paul's company report to the Company Commander. They had gone up to the front with 150 men and their Commander is distraught to discover that only 32 have returned.

CHAPTER 7

The greatly depleted company needs reorganising and they are sent far back behind the lines. Himmelstoss has become less arrogant and wants to make friends. Paul is receptive to this because it was Himmelstoss who rescued Haie Westhus and brought him back to the trenches. Tjaden is less willing, but changes his mind when Himmelstoss becomes the cook and gets the men easy work in the cook-house, providing them with extra food. They are all quick to forget their experiences of recent days: in fact they know that they *must* forget, because to dwell on such thoughts is too destructive.

Kropp and Paul find a poster of a beautiful young girl and are amazed that such loveliness can still exist. Their desire for female company is obvious, as is their innocence and they decide that, in order to appeal to a girl like that, they should at least go and get de-loused!

During the evening, the men go swimming in the nearby canal, observed by three French women, from one of the houses opposite. Although the men are not allowed to cross to the other side of the canal, they arrange to meet that night at the girls' house and promise to bring food with them. When it is dark Paul, Kropp and Leer set off on their adventure, where they succumb to their pent-up desires.

Paul is given seventeen days leave and informed that, afterwards, he must go to a training camp. He will not return to his company for six weeks and Paul wonders whether all of his friends will still be alive when he gets back.

After a long journey, Paul reaches his home town and finds its landmarks unchanged. He is reminded of his youth, and the time he spent here with his schoolfriends, who are either dead or still at the front. When he gets to his own home, he is so overcome with emotion that he weeps when he hears his sister's voice. His mother, who is ill in bed, is anxious that his unexpected arrival means he must have been wounded, but when she learns that this is not the case, they plan to cook Paul's favourite meal. Paul finds that these, once familiar surroundings, now seem strange.

He has brought some food supplies with him and his mother and sister, Erna, are grateful for them: food is in short supply. His mother asks what is is like at the front and, knowing that she could never understand the truth, Paul lies and tells her that the rumours she has heard are unfounded. Paul decides that, at least in front of his mother, he must control his thoughts, emotions and responses. He leaves her to get up and goes to talk to Erna, who tells him that their mother's illness is cancer.

Later on, Paul goes to report to the district commandant. On his way back home, he is confronted by an arrogant major, whom he had failed to salute. Although Paul points out that he has only just arrived from the front, the blustering major delights in humiliating him. When he gets home, Paul changes out of his uniform into civilian clothes. He feels strange to be out of uniform, but his mother is pleased because he seems more familiar to her. Paul's father would prefer him to stay in uniform, however, so that he can show his son off. He wants Paul to tell him details of what the war is like, failing to understand that battle is not adventurous. Paul escapes the confines of his home, but is almost as disturbed by the outside world: he becomes frightened by the noise of tramcars, which sound like shells. Then he is accosted by his former German master, who also asks too many questions. Paul is taken by this man to a bar, where he unwillingly sits and listens to the locals, whose opinions of the war differ greatly from the reality. Eventually he manages to escape these bar-room politicians.

As his leave progresses, Paul feels more and more isolated. He knows that his experiences at the front have changed him and he cannot understand the complacency of the people at home. Even in his old room, surrounded by his beloved books, he cannot recapture the life and feelings that he had before the war. He tries to console himself that it might be easier once the war is over.

Paul goes to visit another old schoolfriend, Mittelstaedt, who had been wounded and now trains territorials at the barracks. Mittelstaedt gleefully tells Paul that their former teacher, Kantorek, has been called up and is under Mittelstaedt's command. By way of revenge for the many classroom humiliations and for goading the boys into enlisting, Mittelstaedt enjoys persecuting Kantorek, comparing him unfavourably with another territorial, Boettcher, who had been the school porter. Kantorek has tried reporting Mittelstaedt to his superiors, but to no avail.

His leave passes quickly and eventually Paul must go and visit Kemmerich's mother. She is distraught and wants Paul to give her the details of her son's death. He lies and says that Kemmerich was killed instantly. She does not believe Paul until he swears on his own life that he is telling the truth.

During Paul's final night at home, his mother creeps into his room. They talk and Paul is reminded of his youth: he longs for his lost innocence and the safety of childhood. His mother is worried about him and he tries to placate her by saying that he will get a job that keeps him out of danger. He takes his mother back to her own room, but once he has returned to his own bed, he is overcome with grief. This life does not belong to him anymore and, discovering that it still exists in his absence, makes him wish that he had never come home.

CHAPTER 8

At the training camp, Paul finds it easier to spend his rest-time alone, although he takes the opportunity to observe the countryside. Next to the camp is a Russian prison camp, whose prisoners are so hungry that they are forced to beg and forage for food in the rubbish from the training camp. Paul observes how similar these men are to German peasants - they do not look like an enemy - just like normal men. Paul has to guard the Russians and, although he wants to sympathise with them, he knows that if they were free, he would try to kill them and they him. As it is, he avoids being cruel and tries to focus on what it would be like if these men were not his enemy. Many of the Russians die and Paul observes their funerals. He hears their music and it makes him sad.

Paul is not allowed any leave, so his father and sister visit him before he returns to the front. They tell him that his mother is in hospital, but that she cannot be operated on until they know what the cost will be. Paul pities his father, who will have to work extra hours to raise enough money for the operation and after-care. When they leave, they give him some potato-cakes - his favourite dish. Although he does not really want them, he eats them because his mother made them, but he also shares some with the Russians.

CHAPTER 9

Paul returns to his company and is eventually reunited with his friends. He is relieved to be back amongst people who understand him. There is a rumour that they are going to be posted to Russia, and the men receive new kit. After a while they discover the truth: they are not going to Russia, but are going to be inspected by the Kaiser. After many preparations, the Kaiser arrives. His appearance is a disappointment to Paul, who had expected him to be a larger man than he is. Afterwards Paul and his friends discuss the war and its origins and they agree that it serves no purpose. Later, they have to give back the new kit, which had only been given to them because of the Kaiser's visit.

The men are sent back to the front line again. On the way they pass a scene of devastation and Paul sees something which is new to him: men who have been blown out of their clothes by trench-mortars. They seem to have become separated from their clothing, right down to their underwear. When the men get to the front, Paul volunteers to go on a patrol into No Man's Land. Once out there in the darkness, Paul becomes frightened by a shell which lands close by him. He begins to panic and in his fear becomes paralysed. He knows that he cannot remain in a shell-hole indefinitely yet is terrified of leaving it and facing the unknown. Suddenly, however, he realises that he can hear the voices of his comrades and regains control. He hauls himself out of the shell-hole and starts to make his way back towards his own trench. All of a sudden, he senses that he is lost - he has no idea where his own lines are. Then, without warning, a bombardment begins and he is forced to take shelter in another shell-hole.

Paul decides that when the expected attack begins, he will pretend to be dead, but as the soldiers pass overhead, he grabs hold of his dagger to protect himself if someone should decide to join him in the shell-hole. He listens to the sounds of battle overhead and it soon becomes clear that the enemy attack is failing and they must retreat. Just as Paul begins to think they have all passed him by, a man slips over into his shell-hole. Without thinking or hesitating, Paul stabs this man. Afterwards, when his fear has subsided, he creeps as far away as possible from the dying soldier, but the gunfire is still too fierce for him to leave.

In the morning, Paul gets his first glimpse of the enemy soldier and crawls over to his side of the shell-hole. The soldier is initially terrified, but when he realises that Paul wants to help him, he calms down. Paul climbs down to the bottom of the shell-hole to gather water, which he strains through his handkerchief before giving it to the dying soldier. Then he tries to bandage the man's wounds, although he knows that nothing can prevent his death.

Watching this man die slowly is torture and Paul wishes that he had his revolver and could shoot him and put them both out of their misery. Eventually, at about three o'clock in the afternoon, the man dies. Paul begins to think about the man's family and his own fate. He feels as though he is losing control. He realises that this man is not really very different from him and he asks for forgiveness. In his confusion, he makes all sorts of promises to the dead man. Then he finds the man's pocket book and discovers photographs of his family and that the man's name had been Gérard Duval and that he had been a printer. Again, he promises that he will take care of Duval's family; that he will become a printer. He knows, however, that he is only making these promises to ease his own conscience.

As the day progresses, Paul becomes calmer, although hunger and tiredness are beginning to take their toll. He is vaguely aware of the approaching dusk and suddenly the will to survive overwhelms him. With renewed vigour, he climbs out of his shell-hole: Duval and his promises are forgotten as he creeps back towards his own front-line trenches. He calls out and is answered by Kat who, together with Albert Kropp, has been preparing to go out and search for Paul. While he eats, Paul explains his absence, but reveals nothing about Duval.

By the next morning, Paul decides to tell Kat and Albert about Duval. They comfort him, telling him that he had no choice. They point out one of their comrades - a sniper named Oellrich - who is delightedly picking off enemy soldiers. Paul decides that his friends are right: there is nothing to be gained by dwelling on his experience - it is best forgotten.

CHAPTER 10

The men are sent to guard a nearby abandoned village which houses a supply dump. They relish this duty as they are able to make themselves quite comfortable in a cellar and they find food, including two sucking pigs, eggs and fresh vegetables from a nearby field. As they are cooking this feast, however, the smoke from the fire is seen by an observation balloon. Shells begin to fall around them, but they continue cooking until everything is ready. Now they must risk their necks and get themselves and the food back to the safety of their cellar. Once there, they enjoy a hearty feast, and then a little later, they eat yet more. Eventually all of this rich food takes its toll on their stomachs.

While guarding this village they also raid the supply dump, giving bread and tinned food to passing drivers, who would have taken the food anyway, had the village been unguarded. This way, however, Paul and his friends are able to trade food for things that they need. The men enjoy this luxurious lifestyle for a few weeks, eating, drinking and befriending an abandoned cat. Eventually, however, they receive orders to evacuate another village. They pile food, cigarettes, furniture and the cat into two lorries and set off.

As they march towards this village, they are passed by evacuating civilians, leaving their homes and taking only what they can carry. Suddenly a shell lands nearby. The men try to take cover, but Paul quickly realises that he and Albert Kropp are too exposed. He feels something strike his left leg and hears Albert cry out. The two men get up, despite their injuries, and run towards a hedge, which they manage to clamber over and they land in a ditch on the other side. Paul drags Albert on, unwilling to leave his friend behind, despite his obvious pain. Eventually, after much running, they reach a dugout where Paul bandages Albert's damaged knee. Albert does the same for Paul, who spots a passing ambulance and manages to raise the alarm. They are taken to a dressing station, where pain finally catches up with them. They manage to stay together and Albert tells Paul that if the doctors remove his leg, he will kill himself.

Paul's wound is cleaned up and he is told that he will be going home the next day. He and Albert bribe the medical sergeant-major to let them stay together during the train journey. The next day, they are taken to the railway station on stretchers. It is pouring with rain and although the sergeant-major covers them over, they are soaked through by the time they are put into the train. Kropp is placed on a lower bunk and Paul is told to climb onto the bed above. At first he is embarrassed because his clothes are dirty and full of lice, while the bed is neatly made up with fresh white sheets. One of the nurses reassures him that this does not matter. They pay off the sergeant-major and before long, the train starts.

During the night, Paul wakes up because he needs to use the toilet. While trying to get out of bed, however, he falls to the floor. The nurse enters the carriage and helps him back into his bunk. Once again, Paul is too embarrassed to say why he was trying to get out of bed and eventually Albert comes to the rescue and explains all to the nurse who fetches a bottle for Paul to use.

After three days of travelling, Paul is told that because Albert has a fever, he will be taken off the train at the next stop. Desperate not to be parted from his friend, Paul manages to fake a high temperature himself and both men are taken to a Catholic hospital at the next station. The next morning Paul is woken by the nuns praying outside the door of the hospital ward. He asks them to close the door, but when they refuse, he throws a bottle in their direction and they relent. Later, when the hospital inspector visits, he asks who has done this. Before Paul can confess, another man interrupts and says it was him, but points out that he has a certificate stating that he is not responsible for his own actions. The inspector leaves because he is not allowed to punish this man - Josef Hamacher

Of the eight men in the room, one - named Peter - has a badly wounded lung. Another, Franz Wächter, has an injured arm. One night, Franz cries out in pain, asking for help. Paul rings his bell, but no-one comes. Eventually the night-sister appears: Franz has suffered a haemorrhage. By the next morning he looks seriously ill. Then he is taken away and does not return. Josef explains that Franz would have been taken to the Dying Room - a place where those for whom there is no hope are taken, partly because it is nearer to the mortuary and partly so that the other men do not have to witness each and every death. Later that afternoon, there is a new patient in Franz's bed, although he too disappears within a few days. Thus it goes on.

A few days later, Peter is removed. He guesses where they are taking him and vows to return to the ward. Once Peter has gone Josef reveals that no-one has ever come back from the Dying Room. Two young soldiers arrive and the surgeon notices that they have flat feet, stating to them that he can 'cure' them. Despite their reluctance and Josef's entreaties, the surgeon gets his own way and operates.

Albert's leg has been amputated and he has fallen into a deep depression. Paul is worried about his friend. Another man tries to commit suicide by stabbing himself through the heart with a fork. Eventually, the Dying Room becomes redundant, as the men are dying too quickly to be moved. On a more positive note, Peter returns to the ward, weak, but triumphant that he has been proved right.

Paul is allowed to get out of bed and make use of crutches but finds this difficult, as Albert constantly watches him, so he goes into the corridors and hobbles around, looking into the other wards. He realises now how many wounded and dying men there are. He ponders on the futility of the war.

There is a man in Paul's ward named Lewandowski, who has had a severe abdominal wound. He has already been in hospital for ten months, but is very excited because he has received a letter from his wife, saying that she is going to visit with their child, whom Lewandowski has never seen. Unfortunately this excitement proves too much and Lewandowski develops a fever which confines him to bed. This threatens to ruin his plans. He has not seen his wife for two years and he had planned that, during her visit, he would find a quiet place, away from the ward, for them to make love. Now he is distraught and the others try, in vain, to console him. When his wife, Marja, arrives the men hatch a plan: two men stand guard by the door, Albert takes charge of the child and the rest play cards noisily while Lewandowski makes love to his wife. Afterwards, she shares out the sausages which she brought for her husband and any embarrassment is soon forgotten.

Soon, Paul is well enough to go home to convalesce. He hates parting from Albert, who is slightly better but still does not talk very much. When he gets home he finds his mother very unwell, but all too soon he gets orders to return to the front.

CHAPTER 11

Back at the front, Paul ponders upon how meaningless his life has become. He now believes that the only certainties in war are death and comradeship. He knows that the alterations to his own character are temporary, yet he clings to them for survival. He recalls the story of his friend Detering. The sight of cherry blossom had made Detering feel homesick and he had tried to escape and go home. Paul reflects that no court martial would ever understand a man's desire to see his home again. He remembers another man, Berger, who had bravely manned a machine gun while his comrades regrouped, but later had been badly wounded trying to rescue a stranded dog from No Man's Land.

Müller dies after being shot in the stomach by a Verey light. He lives long enough to pass Kemmerich's boots on to Paul. The soldiers sense that they are losing the war - they are outnumbered since the Americans have arrived; they do not have enough food, guns or aeroplanes. Many of them are ill due to malnutrition. They begin to think that Germany will soon run out of men, although many who should not be passed fit are still being sent back to the trenches to face artillery fire, and worst of all, tanks.

During an attack the Company Commander, Bertinck, is killed. He had been trying to kill a man who had been using a flame-thrower, but had been shot himself. His first wound is in his chest, but later a shell fragment smashes his chin and passes beyond him, tearing open Leer's hip. Leer soon dies from loss of blood. Paul reflects bitterly that no amount of education will benefit his friend now.

As the summer of 1918 passes, Paul realises that the war is lost and seems confused about why the fighting continues. As the flowers bloom, he hears rumours of an armistice and his lust for life begins to rise. Like many others, he hopes and prays that he will not be killed so near the end. The lack of men and supplies takes its toll, however, and when coupled with the rain, life seems very unfair.

One day, Kat is shot in the leg. Paul knows that his friend needs help quickly and carries him on his back towards the nearest dressing station. Eventually the shelling gets too heavy and they are forced to take shelter in a shell-hole. Here they talk for a short while until Kat's condition worsens and they are forced to go on. When they finally reach the dressing station, Paul is exhausted, but relieved: Kat is safe. Then an orderly tells him that he has wasted his energy - Kat is dead. Paul refuses to believe it, until he spots a small wound on Kat's head, where a splinter has penetrated. Everything seems as it was before, except that now Paul is alone - all of his friends are gone.

CHAPTER 12

Time has moved on and it is now autumn. Paul believes that if peace does not come soon, there may be a mutiny. He has been sent to rest, having inhaled some gas. He longs for peace and yearns to go home, but cannot think about what he will do when he gets there. He feels lost - his generation will be always isolated by their experiences. He hopes that this feeling will pass once he goes home and realises that he will not have to fight again. He is no longer afraid of the future, but feels strong enough to face it and take whatever comes his way.

FOOTNOTE

Paul died in October 1918 on a quiet day. His face was calm: he did not die in pain, but it would seem, was grateful that, for him, the fight was finally over.

Character Analysis

PAUL BÄUMER

At the beginning of the story, Paul is 19 years old. He has been at the front for some time - certainly long enough to have become an experienced soldier, but also long enough to lose his innocence and become more critical and cynical about the war. Before enlisting, he had been a student, who wrote poetry and had begun writing a play. He had a room at his parent's home, which he filled with books, pictures and drawings. Like many of his friends, he had been quite studious, spending his evenings working on his poems.

Paul and his schoolfriends, Kemmerich, Müller, Leer, Kropp and Behm, together with the rest of their class, had enlisted following pressure from their schoolmaster, Kantorek. Behm had been reluctant to join up but had yielded to the pressure and gone along with the others. He had been the first to die and, although it would be easy to blame Kantorek for this, Paul does not. He has come to understand that Kantorek merely represents so many others at home, who were happy to use any means at their disposal to goad young men into doing their perceived duty. Such attitudes have made Paul bitter - any patriotic fervour he may once have felt has been trampled into the mud.

Kemmerich's death, although moving and having an emotional impact on Paul, actually seems more to reinforce his view that the war has numbed him to events which would, in the past, have devastated him. He has already seen so much death and suffering and this parting from his old friend serves to demonstrate the waste of human life that the war has become. Paul is angry because he cannot understand why Kemmerich has to die, yet he also knows that there is nothing he can do.

Despite his anger, Paul can still feel and show sympathy and kindness for his fellow soldiers. He offers help and advice to new recruits, whose lack of experience and training makes them easy targets during raids. This is particularly well demonstrated when the men go out to lay barbed wire (Chapter 4). Paul shelters a young recruit during the bombardment that follows, cradling the terrified young man in his arms. When it becomes clear that the recruit has been so frightened that he has soiled his underpants, Paul is sympathetic - he does not mock, but gives the recruit useful advice and tries to reassure him.

Paul is a thoughtful young man, who often takes time to reflect upon the turn his life has taken and the changes which have been forced upon him. In Chapter six, following an assault, he is on sentry duty and takes this time to think about his life. Thoughts of his childhood, such as sitting with his friends at the side of a stream, flanked by poplar trees, make him realise that he *needs* these calm thoughts and memories to counteract the noise and horror of his current surroundings, where there seems to be no escape from the suffering. Such memories, however, always result in a deep sadness for his lost youth and innocence. They also serve to remind him that his future is bleak.

This is a common train of thought for Paul. He firmly believes that the men of his particular generation are lost. They had not had the opportunity to really experience life before they enlisted, and their futures will always been clouded by their participation in the war. He feels as though he has lost the ability to feel or care about anything other than his comrades and survival: it is as though he cannot afford to waste the energy thinking about other matters, as they are no longer of any importance.

Paul has gained, through bitter experience, a strong sense of what is required for a man to survive in the trenches. He has developed an ability to separate his feelings from his actions. Up at the front, he and his comrades know that they must either kill, or be killed; they see their friends killed or wounded, but when there is no longer anything that can be done for these men, they seem to be able to move on and continue with their own lives. They do this because they have to. Paul knows that it is useless to dwell on events that cannot be altered or helped. He also appreciates that this is why the men resort to humour when they are behind the lines - not because they have forgotten their dead friends, but to remind themselves that they are still alive - at least for the moment.

As the story progresses, Paul's feelings do not necessarily change as such, but they deepen. This is particularly so after his visit home, during which he witnesses the attitude of civilians at first-hand. He refuses to allow his father to show him off, in uniform, to his friends, because he feels that this would force him to demonstrate a false pride in what he has become. Paul's encounter on the street with a blustering major also fuels his anger, that this man - another soldier - is obviously so inexperienced in the realities of the war, that he thinks it is still of paramount importance that Paul should salute him. The major makes no allowance for Paul's tiredness or war experiences, but admonishes him, somewhat ridiculously, for having poor manners and a lack of discipline.

Eventually, before he returns to the front, Paul's sadness becomes more and more intense and he begins to wish that he had never come home. Seeing his mother, especially as she is so unwell, makes him regret that he gives her cause to worry further. He finds it difficult to reconcile his own experiences with the conversations in bars and cafés in which he is forced to become involved. It is as though, even here, he cannot escape the war as almost everyone seems to have an opinion on the fighting, the progress of the war and how matters should be moved forward. One such conversation even leads to Paul being told that he knows nothing about the war and that the man concerned lives in expectation of hearing that Paul has done something worthwhile. Paul feels jealous of the ignorance of such men: he wishes that he did know nothing about the war. He also struggles to understand how these men can be satisfied with their lives, while a war is being fought, on their behalf, by others.

This visit home makes him realise, more than anything else, how much the war has changed him. His efforts to make a connection with his old life prove fruitless and he finds more solace in thinking about his comrades at the front than in anything else he experiences while on leave. Reminders of his childhood, such as his books and the short trousers hanging in his wardrobe, serve only to reinforce his pre-existing thoughts that he had not been much more than a child when he enlisted and that, no matter what happens, that time can never be regained. He has lost his youth, his innocence and his ambitions.

By this time, Paul seems to be almost indifferent as to his own fate: nothing seems to matter much anymore. This is demonstrated by his willingness to swear on his own life, to Kemmerich's mother, that her son died instantly. His life means that little to him now.

When he is at the training camp, especially when he is guarding the Russian prisoners, he begins to contemplate the ridiculous situation in which he has found himself: he must guard men, who, if they were free, would kill him. He cannot see these men as his enemy and yet immediately he understands that for him to think this way is dangerous to his own survival. This realisation does not prevent him from showing small kindnesses to the Russians - he gives them cigarettes and potato cakes which shows that he still maintains a sense of humanity despite his experiences. These men, like him, would rather not be at war, but given that they are, Paul can see no reason to forget that he is capable of consideration for a fellow-sufferer.

Paul's return to the front and the ensuing events, demonstrate that war-weariness is starting to have an effect on him. During a night patrol, Paul becomes frightened by a shell that lands unexpectedly close to him. He shelters, terrified, in a shell-hole, too frightened to move, until he hears familiar voices which remind him of his comrades. This reawakens one of his strongest emotions, and certainly the most positive one to come out of the war - his love for his friends. This makes him feel strong again and he regains a belief in himself. Later on, he is unsure which is the way back to his own trench and it is during this time that the enemy launches an attack and a French soldier falls into Paul's shell-hole. Paul stabs this man - Duval - and must then sit and watch him die. Paul tries to ease Duval's passing - he fetches water and dresses his wounds, although even he is unsure exactly why he is doing this. He believes it might be because he feels guilty, and also in the hope that should they be discovered by other enemy soldiers, he will be able to plead for mercy, by showing that he has tried to help their comrade. This whole episode shows that Paul's sense of survival has returned. Once Duval has died, he makes bargains with the dead man, that if he should be allowed to live, he will write to Duval's wife, send her money, even become a printer. As the time passes, he realises that he will do none of these things and that he was only saying them to ease his own conscience. He waits for the cover of darkness so that he can try to find his way back. His will to live has resurfaced and he manages to overcome all his other thoughts and fears in order that he can return to his comrades.

This love for his friends is now Paul's abiding solace. When he and Kropp are wounded, he is desperate that they should not be separated: he drags Kropp to safety and instigates the bribing of the sergeant-major to ensure that they can be kept together. However, when Kropp's leg is amputated, Paul is unable to offer words of consolation to his friend, as he had previously done to Kemmerich, because he now understands that such words are meaningless. Paul seems to feel guilty that a similar fate has not befallen him and he avoids Kropp's gaze by taking his exercise in the hospital corridors.

The episodes following his injury help to demonstrate Paul's youth and inexperience - not of war, but of life. Despite all of his experiences at the front, he cannot bring himself to ask a nurse for help with going to the toilet. She represents a reminder of his own innocence, unlike the women who had featured in the episodes in the house by the canal. The brunette who had relieved Paul's desires had disappointed him - she had not been really interested in him, but in his 'adventures' and did not live up to his naive expectations, which had been fuelled by a poster of a wholesome young girl.

Paul is saddened by the changes in his friend, Kropp, who remains quiet and sullen. Parting from him is difficult, but Paul knows that it must be done and, by now, he has lost so many friends, he has become accustomed to leaving and to being left. One by one, Paul's friends continue to die, conditions worsen and the war seems hopeless. Paul becomes even more aware of the waste and futility of his existence until he is called upon to carry the wounded Kat on his shoulders to a dressing station. This action, he feels, is an honour - here, at last, is something worth doing. The crushing disappointment of discovering that Kat is dead is the final blow to Paul's senses: he no longer feels anything.

Now that Paul is alone, he senses that he has nothing left to lose: the war has taken everything - his youth, his innocence, his friends. He is unsure what the future holds, but retains a small hope that, somehow, he may be able to regain something of his old self. At no time does despair completely overwhelm Paul: even in his darkest moments, he seems able to clutch at some ray of hope - no matter how distant. These hopes are not born of his circumstances or experiences, but of his own will, which, at the very end of the story, he refuses to acknowledge can have been completely crushed.

The only part of the novel which Paul does not narrate is the event of his own death. The impression given here is that Paul was relieved to die; that this was an easier option than living with the uncertainty of the future, and that finally he had found peace. There is a touch of irony in this final statement: that Paul, who had lived a very short, but tempestuous and ruined life, should die in a relatively peaceful way, on an unusually quiet day, so close to the end of the war that had taken everything from him.

STANISLAUS KATCZINSKY

Kat, as the men call him, is the oldest of Paul's group of friends, at forty years of age. Experience and wisdom make him the natural leader of this group. Paul believes that, before the war, Kat had been a cobbler, but also believes that his occupation would have been irrelevant as Kat demonstrates a sound knowledge of many things, which earns him the respect of his fellow soldiers. He has a sixth-sense: he can tell when something is going to happen - whether that be a storm or a bombardment. He also has an ability to find food and supplies for himself and his comrades, even in the most difficult circumstances.

Kat and Paul seem to be close friends and Paul looks up to Kat, respecting his opinions. In fact, when Paul becomes frightened in No Man's Land, while on a night patrol (Chapter 9), it is his belief that he can hear Kat's voice which reminds him of his comrades and makes him determined to find his way back. Also, when Paul does get back to the trench, he is met by Kat who, together with Albert Kropp, had decided to venture out in search of their missing friend. The next day, when Paul reveals that he has killed Duval, Kat is on hand with words of wisdom and reassurance.

Kat has a dry, dark sense of humour, although more often than not, his humourous remarks have a sense of grim reality about them. This demonstrates his wisdom and his maturity - he understands that nothing around him makes any sense, but he also knows that there is no point in trying to change it. He feels the best solution is to make the best of each situation in which he finds himself. Thus, he is always looking out for the best billets, the easiest jobs and extra food, which he always shares with his comrades.

Kat shows, during conversations with the others, that he is a thoughtful man. For instance, whenever they discuss the war, whether in terms of its causes or its conduct, his answers are always measured. Good examples of such conversations can be found in Chapters nine and eleven. His responses during their discussion following the Kaiser's visit show that the cause of the conflict is a subject on which he has thought a great deal. He also shows his maturity here: he might have less to say than his younger, more effusive comrades, but his comments are more calm and sensible.

In Chapter five, when Kat shows his friends a photograph of his wife, he returns it to his pocket-book, cursing because the war has caused him to be separated from his family. Even here, though, his thoughts are of a practical nature, as he is concerned about ensuring that his family are well fed.

When Kat is wounded, Paul does not hesitate to carry him back to a dressing station. In one of their moments of rest, we learn that Paul is actually returning a favour: Kat had carried Paul in the same way, three years earlier. The comradeship between these two is most obvious in this scene as Paul admits to himself how lonely he will be without his friend.

ALBERT KROPP

Like Paul, Albert is 19 years old at the beginning of the story. He is one of Paul's schoolfriends, described as someone who can think clearly. Paul ironically assumes that this clarity of thought has held Albert back as far as promotion is concerned, implying that he would already have risen much further in the ranks, had he been less intelligent or outspoken.

Albert obviously feels strongly about the suffering and conditions of the ordinary soldiers. For example, he reacts violently to an orderly at the hospital, who initially refuses to give Kemmerich a dose of morphia. Kropp angrily accuses this man of treating officers better than the men. Albert had also stood up to Himmelstoss during training, by calling his bluff when he had threatened to report himself and Paul for tipping a bucket of sewage over his legs. These episodes demonstrate Kropp's sense of injustice and his willingness to do something about it.

Kropp has a realistically pessimistic view of the war. While the others discuss what they will do when the war is over, Kropp refuses to acknowledge that such a time will ever come. He can see no future for himself or his friends because they have no life to return to - they had barely begun to live before the war, but now their experiences will always cloud their thoughts, desires and ambitions. He does not say that the war has ruined everything, but that it has ruined *them* to the point where nothing can exist for them, except the war itself.

When Himmelstoss arrives at the front, again Kropp stands up to him, sensible of the injustice that this man, who has no knowledge of trench-life, should think himself superior to experienced soldiers. He knows that his outburst will probably be punished, but realises that this way, Himmelstoss can be stopped for good - that once he has been censured by the company commander, he will no longer have any power over the men.

Whenever the men discuss the war, Albert demonstrates that its origins and conduct are subjects of great interest to him. He seems more mature than many of his friends, as he tries to see events from more than just his own perspective. Like the others, however, his attempts to make sense of the war are always futile.

When he is wounded in the leg, Albert tells Paul that he will kill himself, rather than live without a leg. Paul manages to ensure that he and Albert are always together and once Albert's leg has been amputated, he initially repeats his threat before turning to silence. Once Paul can move about, he becomes aware that Albert looks at him differently. The reader senses that Albert resents Paul for still having all his limbs and possibly that he feels jealous. He may also feel angry that Paul bothered to save him and keep them together - he would rather be dead and Paul now reminds him of everything that he has lost. As time passes, the sadness never really fades from Albert, whose former personality has diminished as he merely observes the others, rather than joining in. The removal of his leg has a greater impact than just the physical loss.

CORPORAL HIMMELSTOSS

Described as a small man, in every sense of the word, Himmelstoss had been the corporal responsible for training Paul and his friends in preparation for them going to the front. Himmelstoss is universally disliked because he had been far more harsh during training than was necessary and had delighted in punishing the men for any misdemeanour, no matter how insignificant. A proud, self-satisfied man, Himmelstoss continues to rule with a rod of iron at the training camp, until one day he oversteps the mark and is sent to the front.

When he first arrives, he tries to exert his authority over Paul and his friends, but they are having none of it. At the front, it is experience that counts, and the men soon make it clear that they have no time for Himmelstoss and his rules and regulations. Having lost his authority, Himmelstoss is forced to behave more humanely towards the men.

The reality of warfare comes as quite a shock to Himmelstoss and during his first spell in the front lines, he reacts badly, cowering in a dugout, while the others, including the younger new recruits, go over the top. Nothing that Paul says or does can shake his fear and he only moves when ordered to do so by a senior officer. Paul notes, however, that this order acts like a catalyst, changing Himmelstoss from a cowardly wreck to a courageous man almost instantly. It is as though he is only capable of responding to authority - he must be told exactly what to do by someone whom he can respect.

From this moment on, Himmelstoss is a changed man - he has demonstrated both courage and humanity by rescuing Haie Westhus from No Man's Land and now he wants to be friends with Paul and the others. One also senses that he wants to make amends for having treated them so badly in the past. Once he is assigned the role of cook, he gets extra treats for the men and arranges kitchen duties for them, ensuring that they receive better food. This demonstrates how naive Himmelstoss had been: until he had experienced the terror of a battle, he had no real understanding of what he was training recruits for; afterwards, it seems he feels guilty, both for his lack of understanding and for his previous treatment of recruits. This shows that, although a proud man, Himmelstoss is capable of admitting that he was wrong - although he does not do so openly - his actions show that he acknowledges his previous mistakes.

KANTOREK

Kantorek had been the boys' schoolmaster in Germany. Full of patriotic fervour, he had goaded the young men into enlisting to fight for their country. His method of persuasion had been to lecture his charges until he eventually wore them down - playing particularly on their sense of duty. His former pupils do not seem to blame Kantorek for his attitude, which had been so common that even their own parents were goading them to join up.

At the beginning of the story, we learn that Kantorek has kept up a written correspondence with Albert Kropp. In this letter, he sends his best wishes to his former students and refers to them as the iron-youth of Germany. These sentiments are difficult for Paul and his friends to hear or understand as they have just watched another former schoolfriend, Kemmerich, dying in a hospital bed. As the story progresses, it becomes harder for the men to associate Kantorek's fine words with their reality.

Eventually, Kantorek is called up as a territorial and is trained by another former student, Mittelstaedt. Unlike Himmelstoss, however, Kantorek still believes he has the upper hand and tries to exert authority over the younger man. When this fails, he reports Mittelstaedt to his commanding officer, but his complaints fall on deaf ears. No-one cares about his position in civilian life and he gets no preferential treatment. It had been easy for him to shame his students into enlisting but now that he is expected to do his fair share, he finds the idea more irksome. Kantorek personifies the worst type of civilian, who still believes himself to be better than the boys he happily sent to do a man's work.

THEMES

WASTE AND FUTILITY

All Quiet on the Western Front is generally acknowledged to be one of the greatest anti-war novels ever written, so it make sense that the futility and waste of war should be one of its main themes. Through the words of the narrator, Paul Bäumer, Remarque displays anger and disillusionment at the human cost of the conflict. He is not just bitter at the deaths and injuries which affected so many, but also at the loss of innocence, hope and ambition, which he feels will forever change the way in which he looks at the world.

There are numerous instances of Remarque's perception that the war is a waste of human lives, which he feels are being mindlessly squandered. He cites the raw recruits who, with little training or understanding of life at the front, are sent to fight and end up throwing their lives away because they lack basic survival skills. Although Paul is not much older than these recruits, his experiences at the front have taught him a great deal, which he tries to pass on to the newcomers. The sort of lessons he has learned, however, are not usual for a man of his age: for example, how to kill a man with a spade because it is more efficient than a bayonet; how to tell the difference between the various types of artillery and how best to avoid them. This 'education' provides a good contrast with his school days, which have so recently and prematurely been terminated. Paul and his comrades have so much experience of death that they have come to accept it as normal.

Paul and his friends often discuss the causes of the war and try to make sense of why it started and why are there. Their conclusion is always the same: they cannot really understand what has happened to them - or why. They have been told so many different versions of the 'facts' behind the conflict, by their parents and others, such as Kantorek, but now they are in the thick of it, they realise that the enemy has been told exactly the same things. They wonder how both sides can be right: how can they all be fighting for good against evil and how can each side claim to have God with them? Their natural conclusion is that it makes *no* sense and to continually try to understand the war is enough to drive a man mad. Remarque frequently points out that in war it does not pay to think too much or too deeply - such thoughts can threaten to a man's best defence - his survival instinct.

The futility of the war is typified by Paul's visit home. Here he sees and experiences food shortages, because all supplies are sent to the soldiers. The concept of fighting to protect his loved-ones must seem incongruous to Paul, when they are in fact, starving in order that the conflict can continue. None of it serves a purpose: food becomes more scarce - even at the front, and soon it becomes clear that the war is lost and nothing has been gained. Paul has lost all of his friends and his only hope is to survive, now that the end is almost here. However, even as he thinks this, he also realises that his future, if he does survive, is uncertain. The war has robbed him of his youth and innocence: he feels isolated, knowing that people at home will not understand what has happened and the far-reaching consequences which will follow from his war-time experiences.

This visit home also teaches Paul that his life has been ruined for good. His past seems like another life, yet everything at home is just the same; it is only Paul that does not fit in. He finds it difficult to imagine ever feeling at home again. Even when he is surrounded by his beloved books, he cannot settle. He hopes that when the war is over, he will feel better, yet throughout the story, he remains unsure.

Such hopeless desperation is difficult to comprehend today, but Remarque manages to capture it in Paul, allowing the reader a glimpse at the desolation caused to the mind of a young man, forced to leave behind everything he had always held dear, to live through the horrific experiences of the First World War. Remarque wrote this novel to try to come to terms with his own participation in the war. As such, one of the most interesting elements of the story is that Paul, unlike Remarque, dies. He meets his end quite calmly, as though he is pleased to finally be released from the torment and confusion that have become his life. This could be an indication that, for Remarque, death might have seemed an easier alternative than facing the unknown in a defeated post-war Germany, with so few friends and nobody left who really understood him or with whom he could share his memories.

COMRADESHIP

In Paul's increasingly difficult and tumultuous world, the comradeship of his fellow soldiers becomes the one positive aspect of his life and the only element upon which he can focus with any degree of satisfaction. Repeatedly, throughout the novel, Remarque reminds the reader, through Paul's thoughts, that despite all of the negative aspects of the war, such as the inhumanity, appalling living conditions and lack of food, there is this one positive: comradeship. This is not mere friendship, such as Paul and his friends had known before the war: it is much more than that.

The feeling which Paul experiences for his fellow soldiers seems confusing. He knows that they would give their lives to save a wounded comrade, yet, once a man is dead, they do not think about him anymore. This is not because these friendships are easily forgotten, but because the survivors sense that it weakens their own resolve to come through the war, if they focus for too long on anything so negative.

Paul had pre-existing friendships with several of the other characters and yet his greatest bond seems to be with Kat, who is twice his age and much more experienced. Paul refers to Kat as the leader of their group and looks up to him. There is a sense of hero-worship in Paul's feelings towards Kat, which can be seen on many occasions throughout the story. One particular episode is the cooking of the goose, where Paul, half asleep, watches Kat basting the bird and feels peaceful and at home with his friend. The love which Paul feels for Kat is not homosexual or physical in any way: it is closer to the love between a son and his father, and yet, in a way it is stronger. Their shared experiences give them a bond which is more unifying than any emotion which Paul has ever experienced before. It is for this reason that Paul feels so exhilarated and relieved when he believes he has managed to save Kat's life. He has struggled to carry his friend back to the dressing station and the discovery that this has been in vain and that Kat is dead, comes as a numbing, devastating blow. Nothing matters to Paul now except the fact that Kat is dead.

Paul's other close friendship is with Albert Kropp, with whom he had been at school. This is a different relationship from the one which Paul shares with Kat: Paul and Albert have more in common such as their shared memories of home and similar levels of experience, both of the war and other matters, like education and women. When they are both injured at the same time, Paul is determined that they should remain together and takes desperate measures to ensure this. After Albert's leg is amputated, however, their friendship changes:

Paul remarks that Albert looks at him differently and that he finds it necessary to exercise in the corridor where Albert cannot see him. It would appear that Albert, whose first thoughts of suicide have faded, finds it difficult to accept that his friend is still 'whole', while he will always be disfigured. Although their parting is difficult, Paul accepts it, as he does with all of his other comrades - except Kat.

In addition to these particular friendships, Paul is also aware of the strength of feeling he and all of his comrades share. They are the only ones who really understand one another - they know when to talk and when to be silent; when to help and when to leave well alone. Within a short space of time these men collectively form bonds which bear comparison with those of long term relationships, such as marriage. They have become able to understand a look or an action, just as easily as a spoken word: they sympathise, they care, they understand, and they love.

COMPLACENCY AT HOME

Almost from the very beginning of *All Quiet on the Western Front*, there is a sense of bewilderment and betrayal towards those at home who should have known better, yet encouraged mere schoolboys to undertake sacrifices which they themselves were not being called upon to make. Paul, ironically states that there would, however, be little point in blaming these people, simply because there are too many of them. The young soldiers have learned, to their cost, that the fine words of their elders count for nothing once the firing starts.

It is not until Paul goes home on leave, however, that the true extent of home-front arrogance becomes clear. In the first incident, Paul meets a pompous major in the street and accidentally fails to salute him. The officer's furious and arrogant response makes Paul go straight home and change from his uniform into civilian clothes. Everywhere he goes, Paul seems to be confronted by arrogance and complacency which make him dread the company of everyone except his mother - the only person who does not ask him any questions, and who is pleased to see him out of uniform.

When Paul meets some of his former teachers, the mens' attitudes sum up the home front reactions in one short conversation. They do most of the talking: in fact the head-master dismisses Paul's contributions, because he believes *he* has a greater understanding of the whole situation than a soldier, who only experiences the war from one perspective. The German-master says that life is harsher for those at home than the soldiers at the front. When they part, the head-master wishes Paul luck and then says that he hopes to soon have some worthwhile news from him. It is no wonder that Paul feels like a stranger in his home town: he senses that he no longer belongs here, where men can be content to sit and talk war and politics, while at the front, others are fighting and dying to protect them. These men talk about the future, but Paul feels that he and his comrades have no future at all; they have no hopes and nothing to come home to.

For this reason, Paul particularly enjoys watching Kantorek's humiliation at the hands of another former schoolfriend, Mittelstaedt. His enjoyment is enhanced by the knowledge that, despite his bluster, there is nothing that Kantorek can do about his treatment. There is a sense of revenge in Paul's tone during this part of the story, which implies that he holds Kantorek responsible, at least in part, for sending him and his friends off to fight. Kantorek, who was once feared and respected, has now become an object of ridicule.

Another aspect of the 'home-front' which is touched upon in *All Quiet on the Western Front* is the attitude of the French women to the soldiers. These women are obviously hungry and agree to entertain the men in return for food. Paul, who is an innocent where women are concerned, seems to read more into this situation than his brunette partner, who quickly loses interest when she hears that Paul is going home on leave. Paul believes that she would be more keen if he was going to fight. Thus, the women in this section are portrayed unfavourably - they are only interested in what they can acquire from the soldiers and hearing about daring exploits and adventures. This is Paul's impression and helps to demonstrate his deteriorating view of civilians.

HORROR OF WAR

In terms of the language used, Remarque holds nothing back in getting across the horrific nature of trench warfare. His descriptions of wounded and dying men are shocking and occasionally sickeningly realistic. For example, in Chapter six, he describes an attack and its consequences: a man whose severed hands are left hanging on the barbed wire; another whose face is removed with the blow of a spade; the expression on a man's face as he is bayonetted in the back. Later, while describing the effects of an artillery attack, the dead are blown apart into so many pieces that, Remarque says, their remains could fit into a mess-tin for burial.

The language he uses in describing men who have no faces; whose intestines are visible through their wounds, who bleed to death because of their terrible injuries, is harsh, realistic and frightening. This is quite intentional. Remarque wanted to provide a graphic portrayal of war - not sanitised or censored, but an explanation of why this war had such a profound effect on his generation. The sights he is describing should never be witnessed by any human being, yet these young men were little more than schoolboys and were expected by their elders, to make sense of this horror.

One of the reasons why Remarque's use of this graphic language is so effective is the contrast that it provides with his descriptions of the men's leisure time. When behind the lines, at rest, Paul notices butterflies, bees, the flowery fields; he feels the wind in his hair. These accounts are markedly different from those of his battle experiences. This helps the reader to appreciate the changes in Paul's life, which he is struggling to come to terms with. A good example of this can be seen in Chapter six. Following an attack, Paul is on sentry duty and in the darkness, he imagines a scene in a cathedral garden, then remembers sitting on a riverbank as a child, dangling his feet in the water beneath him. The language here is serene and calm and contrasts well with the previous description, just a page or two earlier, of the blood-curdling attack from which Paul has just escaped. It also serves to remind the reader of Paul's youth. These childhood memories are still quite fresh to him. The contrast for the reader is compounded when, a few pages later, one of Paul's comrades, Haie Westhus, is fatally wounded. The description of his wounds leaves nothing to the imagination; neither does the account a few lines later, of men who have lost their feet, managing to carry on walking on what remains of their legs, in their desperation to get back to a dressing station, and medical help. The striking difference between Paul's past and his present is evocatively brought to life simply by the use of different forms of language.

COMPARISONS

When students are asked to make comparisons between different novels or poetry, it is often from the perspective of how each author has represented a particular theme or subjects. To that end, we have, where possible, given examples of how authors use different styles and devices within their stories and poems to demonstrate their ideas and themes.

MALE RELATIONSHIPS

The relationships formed by men during the First World War is a common theme in the literature of and about that period. These relationships can range from simple friendship, to hero-worship and to love, whether homosexual or (more commonly) not. There are numerous examples of authors and poets using this theme to demonstrate the humanity of the inhuman events which surrounded men on a day-to-day basis.

One of the most moving poems which deals with this subject is *Comrades: An Episode* by Robert Nichols. In this poem, Nichols makes great use of direct speech, and despite its rhyming couplets, it reads almost like prose. It tells the story of an officer, Gates, who is injured and stranded in No Man's Land. His initial thoughts, that he will die alone, are changed when he hears the voices of his men. This forms an interesting comparison with Paul Bäumer's similar experiences in front of his own trenches in *All Quiet on the Western Front*. Gates resolves that he will get back to his own lines - even if it is only to die - so that he can be with the men he loves so much. Slowly he drags himself back until he reaches the parapet, where three of his men jump up to help him. Two of them are shot and killed, while Gates is pulled down into the trench, distressed that, in trying to help him, they have given their own lives. His men reassure him that the doctor is coming, but Gates dies, his final thoughts and words being of his men. This remarkable poem perfectly captures the bond of comradeship between men serving in the First World War.

Another poet, whose predominant theme was comradeship, was
E. A. Mackintosh, an officer whose overriding qualities were courage, pride and respect for his fellow men. These, together with his love for his men, are themes which feature strongly in his poetry, such as *Recruiting*, in which he suggests that other men should join in the fight - not for King and country, but to discover, as he has, the quality of those with whom they will serve. These men, he says, have honour, courage and dignity and are, as such, so far above the warmongers at home, that the two cannot be compared.

Other novels about the First World War also feature this theme - although not necessarily in the same way as *All Quiet on the Western Front*. *Strange Meeting* by Susan Hill is an interesting example. This novel tells the story of the friendship between two men, John Hilliard and David Barton, which blossoms into love. Unlike the men in *All Quiet on the Western Front*, Barton and Hilliard are officers, thrown together at the front, and as the story progresses they come to rely heavily upon each other. Despite the potential consequences of doing so, they declare their feelings for one another and even begin to make plans for the future together, which is shattered when Barton dies. An obvious difference between these two novels, other than the ranks of the men involved, is that, whether homosexual or not, Barton and Hilliard speak openly about their feelings, whereas Remarque's characters may think, as Paul does, that they love each other, but they do not declare it. In *Strange Meeting*, Hilliard's love for his fellow men is by no means universal, but is restricted to David Barton. By loving Barton, Hilliard's character grows and he becomes more able to understand and communicate with his men, but there is no comparison between this and his feelings for Barton.

In many cases, in fact, the novels of the First World War are written about officers and *their* relationships, rather than the men in the ranks. As such, the officers involved are, for the best part, portrayed as being the products of the public school system, where male friendships and hero-worship would have been quite normal in an environment, essentially devoid of female influences. These relationships are shown as continuing into the trenches, where the division of men into small units guaranteed a sense of brotherhood and camaraderie. A good example of this is R.C. Sherriff's *Journey's End*, in which there are two close friendships. The first is between Stanhope (the senior officer), and Raleigh (a new recruit). These two men had known each other at school, where Raleigh, the younger of the two, had looked up to Stanhope, who was popular, intelligent and a good sportsman. Once in the trenches, Raleigh hopes that their friendship will be as it was before, but is shocked by the change in his former schoolfriend. Three years at the front have taken their toll on Stanhope who now relies - in almost equal measure - on alcohol and Osborne - his second in command. Theirs is the second strong relationship in Journey's End. Osborne declares his love for Stanhope very early in the play, although this is not a homosexual feeling, but one born out of respect and admiration.

Remarque's characters also appear to have come from a male-dominated background: their class at school seems to have consisted entirely of boys and they have grown accustomed to living without women. For the best part, the friendships Paul experiences are just that: comradeship and affection for men and boys, sharing the same horrendous existence. There is one notable exception to this, in Paul's description of Kat as he bastes the goose in Chapter five. Here, he describes the physique of his friend and wonders how Kat would react if anyone should caress him. These thoughts and Kat's presence seem to remind Paul of home, momentarily making him feel safe and he finds, to his surprise, that he is crying.

The different ways in which authors represent this theme are, as much as anything, due to the time at which they were written. Pat Barker in *Regeneration*, for example, speaks of Siegfried Sassoon's love, loyalty and need to protect his men, while also commenting on his homosexuality during his discussions with Dr. Rivers. This book was published in 1991, by which time public attitudes, as well as legal ones, towards homosexuality, were so different from those during the time the book is set, as to be almost unrecognisable. Therefore, Pat Barker is able to discuss homosexual relationships openly. The same applies to all authors whose work was published in the latter part of the twentieth century, or later. The same freedoms did not apply to authors writing in the earlier part of the century, such as Remarque, Sherriff and Sassoon. While these authors could describe their characters' feelings for each other, they must always remain chaste: they could love one another, but it must be a publicly acceptable love - comradeship, not passion.

HOME FRONT

Home front attitudes are another common theme in poetry and prose of the First World War. Many authors use this as a means of demonstrating the bond between the men who are fighting: showing that they now have more in common with each other, than with anything connected with their past lives - including their own families. This theme also serves to reinforce the sense of waste and futility, as the men who return home on leave are seen to become more disenchanted with the cause for which they are supposed to be fighting.

Wilfred Owen, among many others, felt strongly on this point, as is demonstrated in his famous poem, *Dulce et Decorum Est*. This poem was originally subtitled '*to a certain poetess*', and it is generally acknowledged that this was a reference to Jessie Pope (who wrote fervently patriotic verse, goading young men into joining up). The theme of this poem is Owen's anger at those people who continued to propagate the lie that it is 'sweet and meet to die for one's country' - which is a translation of the final two lines of the poem. The language which Owen uses throughout the poem is necessarily shocking and realistic because he is trying to force complacent or arrogant civilians into understanding the real consequences of warmongering. Another of Owen's poems with a similar theme is *Apologia Pro Poemate Meo* (which translates as 'Reason for my Poem'). Here, he describes all the positive elements of the war, such as the discovery of true comradeship in the face of horrendous surroundings, in a poem which is directed at someone safe at home. He finishes by telling this person that, while the soldiers are deserving of a civilian's tears, the civilian is not even worthy of a smile on the face of a serving soldier.

Other popular novels also feature this theme. Among these is *The Return of the Soldier* which was written by Rebecca West in 1918. One of the main characters, Kitty, is portrayed as a shallow, selfish, petty woman, whose sole concern is that the war should not be allowed to spoil her supposedly perfect life. Her husband, Chris, has suffered from shell-shock and lost his memory. The essence of this novel is the debate over whether Chris should be 'cured', which is what Kitty wants, or should be left as he is and allowed to remain safe from the war. Kitty's selfish need for her husband to be returned to her world, takes no account of the fact that he will then have to return to the war and all the horrors which caused his shell-shock in the first place or the possibility that, once there, he may die. West's portrayal of Kitty is harsh and uncompromising - she is shown to be a woman who only cares about herself and her own life and this would seem to represent the author's opinion of home-front complacency. The reader wants and even expects to sympathise with Kitty and yet the personality she has been given makes this impossible. The other characters are portrayed much more sympathetically, which makes Kitty's attitude difficult to comprehend.

In *Regeneration* by Pat Barker, we see a more conventional soldier's attitude to those at home. Billy Prior, who is inclined to think the worst of people anyway, is angered by the way that life, for people at home, seems to be continuing pretty much as it did before the war. On a trip to the seaside with Sarah Lumb, Billy feels out-of-place, surrounded by people enjoying themselves. He questions whether they even know that the war is taking place at all. His anger and resentment become directed towards Sarah, who he feels is more closely connected to the uncaring crowds, than to himself. Pat Barker portrays most of the civilians in *Regeneration* as fairly harsh or shallow characters, which provides a contrast with the officers being treated at Craiglockhart. Civilians are portrayed, for the best part, as less intelligent and more opportunistic - trying to get whatever they can for themselves.

Susan Hill's novel *Strange Meeting* also contains a civilian character whose attitude to the war seems complacent and arrogant. This person is Constance Hilliard, the mother of one of the central characters, John Hilliard. John, at the beginning of the novel, is at home, convalescing. His mother, who is naturally devoid of affection or emotions, is concerned that the family must maintain their standards and appearances. John is made to feel obliged to visit 'the Major', an old retired soldier, full of outdated opinions on how the war should be fought. In addition, John's family are portrayed as failing to understand him; there is a void in their relationship, which John knows cannot be filled. When he leaves home to return to France, his mother, dressed in her finery, escorts him to the station. Upon their arrival there, she comments to John that the stationmaster is failing in his duty to maintain the platform, while pointing out, in passing, that his son has been killed in the war. Constance is portrayed by the author as a cold, heartless woman, whom John is relieved to leave when he returns to the front - where he feels more at home.

All of these works and many others besides, share a common method of portraying the callous, unfeeling and complacent nature of those at home. As previously stated, these civilians are given unfavourable and unflattering characteristics in order to enhance the portrayal of the soldiers and officers who also feature. This device makes the reader more sympathetic towards the serving men and less tolerant of the civilians. In *All Quiet on the Western Front*, Remarque's civilians (with the exception of Paul's mother and sister) are pompous, arrogant and self-opinionated. Eventually, their main representative, Kantorek, is humiliated, when he is made a territorial, but even this does not diminish his authoritarian attitude and he continues to remind Mittelstaedt of their former teacher/student relationship. This treatment is similar to the other authors mentioned above, especially Rebecca West's character of Kitty. Neither of these two personalities can see why the war should affect *their* status or social standing, but have little care of the consequences to others.

It is also interesting to note that neither Kantorek or Rebecca West's Kitty are defeated by the war: if anything the opposite is the case. Kantorek refuses to accept the humiliation of his position and the reader senses that nothing would ever make this man admit that he had been wrong. Kitty also 'wins', in that she gets her own way and Chris's memory is restored, making him, once again, the dutiful husband and soldier. From this point of view, both authors could appear to be saying that arrogance always wins. In *All Quiet on the Western Front*, Paul's entire generation is either killed, maimed, wounded or mentally altered beyond recognition and yet their elders are seen to carry on as before.

The main differences in the treatment of civilians within these pieces stem from the time at which they were written. Owen, Remarque, and to a certain extent Rebecca West had lived through the conflict, although to varying degrees and from different perspectives. Their anger at the home front complacency is therefore more heart-felt and realistic. Susan Hill, Pat Barker and Sebastian Faulks, whose novel *Birdsong* also features this theme, are not writing from first-hand experience, which could explain why their civilian characters seem slightly more stereotyped. Kitty (from *The Return of the Soldier*) and Constance (from *Strange Meeting*) are very similar characters and yet Kitty's selfishness, being such a major feature to the whole plot of Rebecca West's story, makes this characteristic seem of greater importance to the plot and, by extension, to the author.

Another aspect where these authors treat this theme slightly differently is the soldier's reactions to the home front attitude. In *All Quiet on the Western Front*, Remarque portrays Paul as feeling bemused and betrayed. The attitude of the civilians annoys him, but he has come to feel that, compared to his comrades, most civilians are worthless anyway, so their opinions, while infuriating, do not really matter to him and he is simply keen that he should be exposed to them at little as possible. He finds it difficult to feel anything other than contempt for the people he had once respected. In *The Return of the Soldier*, Rebecca West treats this aspect differently, as her soldier, Chris Baldry, has lost his memory. It therefore falls to Jenny, Chris's cousin and the narrator of the story, to express her incredulity at Kitty's selfish attitude. It is only at the end of the story when Chris, the soldier, returns, that the reader gets a glimpse of his real demeanour as he loses his sense of fun and becomes upright and soldierly again. At no time is he angry or bitter about Kitty's attitude, but that is because he has no idea who she is until the very end of the story.

In *Strange Meeting* by Susan Hill, John Hilliard feels lonely and out of place at home, where his mother's life seems to have remained static and untouched by the war. He is incredulous and resentful towards her, but they have always been remote family, not given to displays of emotion, so he keeps his feelings to himself. Billy Prior (in *Regeneration*), and Michael Weir (in *Birdsong*) react in similar ways. Their primary emotion is anger towards complacent civilians. Billy feels as though he wants to make someone suffer for the attitude of arrogant and uncaring civilians whom he encounters and initially he takes his frustration out on Sarah. Eventually, however, he mellows towards her once he realises that she is different from many of the other people at home. Michael Weir, on the other hand, becomes uncharacteristically angry when he returns from leave. His father had been disinterested in hearing about the war, believing that he already had all the information he required from the newspapers. Back in the trenches, Weir relates this to his comrades and becomes increasingly angry and more violent and bitter as he does so, until he can barely control himself.

The portrayals of Billy Prior and Michael Weir, for example, seem more understandable and expected than the quiet bemusement of Paul Bäumer, but that does not make them, necessarily, more realistic. Each person would have reacted differently, depending on their personality, upbringing and relationship with those at home.

WASTE AND FUTILITY

This is one of the most common themes of First World War Literature, whether it was written by those who had first-hand experience, or by more modern authors. *All Quiet on the Western Front* was published in 1929, which is the same year as R. C. Sherriff's play *Journey's End* (although it was first publicly performed in December 1928). Both of these works share this theme - that to the men who lived through it, the war became a pointless, hopeless and needless waste of millions of lives. Both Remarque and Sherriff, together with others, went on to spend many years following the war, trying to reconcile their experiences during the conflict with their lives before and after, and this sense of unnecessary suffering is apparent in both of these pieces.

In *Journey's End*, Sherriff demonstrates the futility of the war in many ways. Among these is his choice of reading matter for Osborne: Alice's Adventures in Wonderland. Trotter is incredulous and mocking, that Osborne should be reading a children's book, and says that he can see no point in it. Osborne simply replies that that is *precisely* why he is reading it. This is a minor conversation which in a small and obscure way reinforces the central theme of futility. *Nothing* makes sense any more, so why should Osborne's book be any different. He agrees with Trotter that it is pointless, but the implication is that everything is pointless.

Another instance of the waste of war, in this play, is the raid in which Osborne dies. Throughout the play, Osborne has been portrayed as the man who holds everyone else together: he protects Stanhope, advises Raleigh and generally speaking, lives up to his nickname of 'Uncle'. Yet Osborne dies so that one young enemy soldier, who is more frightened than knowledgeable, can be captured. This futile exercise has cost the unit one of its best men and Stanhope has lost the only person whom he felt he could genuinely trust.

In *All Quiet on the Western Front*, this theme is a continuous thread, running through the story as gradually, one by one, Paul's friends and comrades are killed. This theme of losing all of one's friends is typified by the passing on of a pair of boots. Kemmerich passes them to Müller, who in turn bequeaths them to Paul, who states that, upon his death, they will be left to Tjaden. The passage of this pair of boots, through so many owners, demonstrates the arbitrary nature of death. This also helps to reiterate the theme of waste in an ironic way: the boots survive, while the wearers perish in turn, until there is no-one left to wear them.

Remarque's other point within this theme is that a man does not have to die, for his life to be wasted. The after-effects for those who survive, he says, will haunt them and invade every aspect of their lives. This loss of innocence is another theme which is shared with *Journey's End*. The character of Raleigh is shown at the beginning of the play to be a young, inexperienced subaltern, whose enthusiasm for joining in the war seems out of place when compared with the war-weary attitude of his old school friend, Stanhope. When Raleigh is selected to go on the raid, he feels that this is an honour, and although he feels nervous, he is also excited at the prospect of seeing some action. After the raid, which costs Osborne's life, Raleigh is unsure how to behave. He cannot understand how Stanhope, Trotter and Hibbert can enjoy a meal together when Osborne has just been killed. This is a difficult experience for Raleigh, although Sherriff demonstrates that the greatest shock of all is the change in Stanhope's personality. Stanhope used to be Raleigh's boyhood hero, but now seems to have rejected him. Raleigh's character reminds the reader, as well as Stanhope, of the older man's own lost innocence and also he does not want his young friend to betray his changed personality to their families at home. Both men appreciate that, even if they survive the war, their relationship can never be the same again.

Some, more modern, authors have also incorporated this theme into their novels. In *Birdsong* by Sebastian Faulks, for example, Jack Firebrace observes the first day of the Battle of the Somme. He is shattered by the scenes he witnesses as more and more men leave the trenches and are mown down by enemy fire. By the end of the day, of the 800 men who had begun the attack, only 155 remain. The roll-call which brings these losses to light is a scene reminiscent of one in *All Quiet on the Western Front*, where a unit of 150 men has been reduced to 32. Both authors use this as a means of demonstrating the sheer number of casualties. In both cases, the officers reading the roll-call react similarly: both are shocked at the decimation of their companies and allow their emotions to show. Remarque's officer speaks quietly and with some difficulty as he issues instructions; while Price, the officer in *Birdsong*, is uncommonly gentle with his men. Both authors also make a point of explaining that there are now fewer men: Remarque does this by stating how much shorter the line of men is, as they walk silently away. Faulks uses a similar explanation, telling us that the remaining men have to line up in a new formation, standing next to strangers, because all the familiar faces have gone.

LANGUAGE

All Quiet on the Western Front contains a great deal of vivid description about the horrendous circumstances in which Paul finds himself. Although other popular authors and poets use strong, uncompromising language to demonstrate this theme, not many do it quite so graphically or realistically as Remarque. As with many of the other themes already discussed, one of the reasons for Remarque's realism is that he experienced the war at first-hand. This is a 'luxury' not afforded to modern-day authors of First World War-based fiction, although in *Birdsong*, Sebastian Faulks has managed to capture the essence of the war through the use of similar language. Like Remarque, he gives graphic portrayals of wounds and injuries, leaving the reader in no doubt as to the horror of witnessing such scenes.

Like Remarque, Sebastian Faulks, also makes use of language to provide a contrast, although his method is somewhat different. Where Remarque provides a contrast between war and peace by using more calm and languid descriptions of more restful times or pre-war memories, Faulks uses similar language in both types of scene. For example, there are marked similarities between his descriptions of battles and injuries and the language he uses when describing sex. Both in the scenes between Isabelle and Stephen and the French prostitutes and Stephen, Faulks uses either the same or similar terms and phrases to those that he employs when describing battle wounds. Although this device is, effectively, the opposite of the one employed by Remarque, the result is the same. By contrasting hideous wounds to the human body, with sexual activity, Faulks forces the reader to compare the two most eventful situations in Stephen's life. This also helps to reinforce, in the reader's mind, the devastating emotional impact which both of these events have on Stephen. His affair with Isabelle is his first experience of love and yet, it transpires, this is a destructive relationship which, despite its intensity, is destined to fail. The war, while initially seeming not to touch his buried emotions, obviously causes him great turmoil, as the reader discovers that, following the Armistice, Stephen did not speak for two years.

While, in both *Birdsong* and *All Quiet on the Western Front*, the use of strong, harsh language serves the purpose of making the battle scenes more believable and provides a contrast or comparison with more peaceful times, it is not always necessary for an author to employ this method in order to achieve a similar result. This can be seen in *Strange Meeting* by Susan Hill, where it soon becomes clear that, in this novel at least, less is more. For instance, when John Hilliard is convalescing at home, he is reminded of the smell of the trenches by the sweet scent of roses which drifts through his open window. This makes him feel physically sick and, although it is the middle of the night, he goes for a walk on the beach, just to escape from this stifling smell. This is an interesting device as Susan Hill's choice of smell - the pungent, heady and overpowering scent of roses in full bloom - is something to which even the modern reader, with no experience of warfare, can relate. She then associates this with the sweet, sickly smell of the trenches - a mixture of blood, gas, earth and chlorine - which helps the reader to understand how this smell comes to haunt John, since everyone can understand the overpowering scent of flowers in a room, which are slightly past their best.

Throughout *Strange Meeting*, there are, of course, descriptions of battle scenes, wounds and dying men, but more often than not, it proves enough to simply say: 'a man was shot', rather than to describe in graphic detail the physical effects of the bullet on his body. The reason that this works so well, in this novel, is that, although the story is set during the First World War, it is not just a story about war: it is, more importantly, a story about love. By maintaining, throughout, an atmosphere of calm, Susan Hill forces the reader to care about the characters and what happens to them. Graphic descriptions of wounds would do nothing to enhance this, and would, possibly, detract from the emotional aspects of the story.

Probably one of the most graphically descriptive poems of the First World War is Isaac Rosenberg's *Dead Man's Dump*. Here, the poet describes the war as a never-ending scene from Hell, where death overpowers everything else and hope and youth are lost forever. He gives realistic portrayals of men with blood splattered faces and bones being crushed, which leave nothing to the imagination, while referring to those who still live as though they are walking dead. No-one *really* lives in this poem which is a realistic portrait of self-destruction and madness.

CHARACTERS

All Quiet on the Western Front is an auto-biographical novel, based on the experiences of Erich Maria Remarque during the First World War. As such, the characters involved are based upon Remarque himself, his friends, comrades and acquaintances and they all serve a purpose: to represent different viewpoints, opinions and attitudes to the war. This device is also used by other authors in this genre.

In *All Quiet on the Western Front*, Paul Bäumer, as the narrator, enables the author to state opinions, without them necessarily appearing to be his own. Paul's voice of lost youth and innocence represents Remarque's own feelings as, following the conflict, he felt as though he had lost everything. Paul's lost ideals and aspirations, mirror Remarque's who obviously survived the conflict, but lost many friends, his ambitions and his mother (who died during the war). Paul is not allowed the 'luxury' of survival and this could demonstrate the author's sense that the war cost him everything, so it may as well have taken his life too.

Rebecca West uses a similar device in her novel, *The Return of the Soldier*. Jenny is the cousin of Chris Baldry, the 'soldier' in the title and she narrates this story. Jenny's character grows throughout the novel, as she gains a greater understanding of her shell-shocked cousin and his life before his marriage, which had always remained a mystery to her. She learns valuable lessons from Margaret, Chris's first love - a working class woman whom Kitty, Chris's wife, treats with disdain. Kitty, a handsome, poised woman, has created a 'perfect' world for herself and her husband and her character represents the outward appearance of beauty. Margaret, on the other hand, is a plain care-worn woman, whose character represents the beauty of the soul. Rebecca West wants the reader, through Jenny, to realise that those, like Margaret, with an inner sense of goodness, are more attractive characters than people like Kitty could ever be.

Besides narrators, other characters also have definite purposes within novels and plays. In *All Quiet on the Western Front*, Detering, for example, is a married farmer, who is homesick most of the time. He rarely speaks and his character serves to remind the reader, as do those of Tjaden and Westhus, that some of these men had built lives before the war. For Detering, this homesickness eventually becomes too much and he tries to escape - not to the safety of Holland, but back to Germany, where he is captured. This shows that he did not just want to escape the war, but actually wanted to go home. His assumed death at the hands of a court-martial serves to further represent the futility of the war. The character of Leer, on the other hand, represents the more street-wise soldier, already experienced with girls and more worldly than is former classmates. However, this wisdom fails to change his fate, as he bleeds to death in a shell-hole.

The play *Journey's End* by R C Sherriff also features similar characters, such as Hibbert who, like Leer, represents the more worldly-wise soldier. Sherriff takes this one stage further, however, by making Hibbert into a cowardly character, whose main aim is to be sent back down the line in order to avoid the anticipated attack. As such, he makes continuous claims of illness, in the hope that Stanhope will order him to be sent for medical examination. This, coupled with his lewd collection of photographs and his comments on the women in them, makes Hibbert an unattractive character. The purpose of him being in the play, other than to demonstrate that such people did exist, is to show Stanhope's nature. Stanhope tries to persuade Hibbert to 'do his duty' - he even threatens to shoot him, and eventually tells Hibbert that he, too, is frightened, but knows that, as officers, they must set an example to the men and support their comrades.

Remarque uses Stanislaus Katczinsky's character to represent the older generation of more experienced soldiers, who were often looked up to by new recruits. For this reason, characters such as Kat are often given the ability of foresight, making them seem even more knowledgeable and wise. Kat provides a father-figure for Paul and the love which forms between them is a strong bond, broken only by Kat's death, which is seen as effectively marking the end of Paul's life, since he feels nothing afterwards.

An obvious comparison with Kat could be Osborne in the play *Journey's End*. He lives up to his nickname of 'Uncle'; he is always on hand with advice for the younger men and is protective of Stanhope. However, an interesting contrast could be made with the character of Stephen Wraysford in *Birdsong* by Sebastian Faulks. Wraysford is not a kindly father-figure, although Brennan (one of his men) later remembers that, while they had all thought Wraysford a little strange, he had shown kindness to a dying man. Michael Weir - another officer and Wraysford's best friend - often asks Wraysford to tell his fortune. For Wraysford this is merely a diversion, but Weir takes it quite seriously and places great importance on Wraysford's predictions. Despite all of his horrific experiences, it is not until Weir dies that the war *really* begins to affect Wraysford. Due to the emotional upheaval of his life before the war, he had never appreciated the value of friendship or love but his friend's death, as well as teaching him this lesson, also makes him understand the depth of his own loneliness.

In *All Quiet on the Western Front*, the company commander, Bertinck, although only having a minor role, is used to show that many of the lower ranking officers were fair, decent men who did their best to look after their men. He dies bravely, saving his men from an oncoming flame-thrower, yet there is a sense of inevitability in his death. Paul points out that, having almost got to the end of the war without being injured, the law of averages dictates that Bertinck should not survive. This character provides a good contrast, within the novel, with that of the blustering Major, whom Paul meets on his visit home. The Major represents inexperienced staff officers, with little or no understanding of the reality of warfare, merely a good knowledge of the rules and regulations which govern the army.

Bertinck's character could be compared with many others. For example: David Barton in Susan Hill's *Strange Meeting*; Siegfried Sassoon, as portrayed in Pat Barker's *Regeneration* or Stanhope in R. C. Sherriff's *Journey's End*. Many authors use a kindly, sensible officer to provide a contrast with the supposedly uncaring attitude of those above them. In *Journey's End*, for instance, Stanhope is dismayed when the Colonel orders that Osborne and Raleigh should lead a raid on the German trenches, in order to capture an enemy soldier so that he may gain information about the opposing troops. He cannot believe that there are no alternative courses available, or that the raid must be made in daylight. The raid costs Osborne's life and gains no significant information, which helps to enhance the perceived wisdom in Stanhope's character.

With the character of David Barton in *Strange Meeting*, Susan Hill takes this one stage further. Initially, Barton's optimistic nature makes the other officers and men feel more at ease and he has an ability to make others like him, without them necessarily knowing why. Then, as he gains experience of the horror and waste of the war, his personality begins to change and he becomes more introverted and retrospective. This story is about the love between Barton and his fellow officer, John Hilliard and it is Hilliard's love which helps him through this difficult time. Although at the time of his death, Barton is still relatively innocent and the war still has many months to run, as with Bertinck, there is a sense of inevitability in Barton's demise. This is not because he has survived for such a long time, or because the law of averages dictates it, but because Barton's death has always been Hilliard's worst fear. His character now must come to terms with the loss of the only person he has ever really loved, and use this experience to build a new life and look forward to the future.

Biography of Erich Maria Remarque

Erich Paul Remark, to give him his real name, was born on June 22nd 1898 in Osnabrück in Germany. His father, Peter, was a bookbinder and together with Paul's mother, Anna Maria, already had one son, Theodor, who had been born two years earlier. Two years after Paul's birth, his sister Erna was born, on September 6th. Just over a year later, tragedy struck, when Theodor died at the age of five. The final child of the family, Elfriede, was born on March 25th 1903. While not poverty-stricken, the family were by no means well-off either and moved several times during Paul's childhood, although they always remained in Osnabrück.

The young Erich attended local schools in the town, before enrolling at the Catholic Preparatory School in 1912. This was a necessary step in his preparation for Teacher Training College. During this time, Erich showed a talent for playing the piano and earned money after school, giving piano lessons. He harboured ambitions of becoming a concert pianist, although he continued with his teacher training, joining the Catholic Royal Teacher Training College in 1915.

Then in 1916, Erich's life changed forever as on November 21st he was conscripted into the German army. Following many months of training, at the Caprivi Barracks in Osnabrück, he was transferred to the Westrn Front, just ten days before his nineteenth birthday, on June 12th 1917.

A few weeks later, on July 31st 1917, Erich was hit by a shell fragment, which caused injuries to his left leg, right arm and neck. He was evacuated to a field hospital. By the end of August, he was well enough to be transferred to a hospital in Duisberg, where, following an improvement in his health, he carried out light duties in the orderly room. While here, on September 9th, he received the news that his mother had died from cancer and was given leave to travel home to attend her funeral a few days later. Although his health continued to improve, he was not passed fit for active service until October 31st 1918, just days before the end of the war. On November 15th, four days after the Armistice, he was presented with the Iron Cross, First Class.

Almost immediately, Erich resumed his education, having been officially discharged from the Army on 5th January 1919. The following month, his father re-married a woman named Maria Bahlmann. Erich qualified as a teacher in June 1919 and took up his first teaching position in August. He did not settle in this profession, however, having three different jobs in the following fifteen months, before deciding to abandon teaching altogether. He then took up a series of odd jobs, including bookkeeper, salesman, piano teacher and organist, although his ambition of becoming a concert pianist never came to fruition due to his injuries in the war.

During his time at Duisberg hospital, he had embarked on his first serious romantic liaison, which ended unsuccessfully. Now that the war was over, he continued to fall in and out of love on a fairly regular basis. He became a journalist and theatre critic and, for the first time, used the name Erich Maria Remarque (Maria in honour of his mother, and the spelling of Remarque being a throw-back to the spelling of his ancestors). Then, in 1922, he moved to Hanover, where he became a copywriter and editor.

Craving a better life, Remarque decided to take up the position of editor at *Sport Im Bild* in Berlin in 1925 and on October 14th of that year, he married Ilse Jutta Zambona, an attractive actress and dancer.

Then in 1927, still traumatised by the First World War, Remarque began work on a wartime novel, the writing of which, he hoped, might help to exorcise some of his demons. In March 1928, he submitted his manuscript, entitled *Im Westen Nichts Neues (All Quiet on the Western Front)*, to the publishing company of S. Fischer, who rejected it. Five months later, it was finally accepted for publication by a company call Ullstein and was initially serialised in a magazine during November and early December. On 15th November Remarque walked out of his job on *Sport Im Bild* and waited for the publication of his novel, which took place in January of 1929.

The following month, Erich began an affair - the first of many during his lifetime. None of his romances prevented him from remaining close friends with Ilsa, despite their divorce in January 1930.

Three months later came the premiere of the film of *All Quiet on the Western Front* - a huge success and winner of Academy Awards. Remarque continued writing, despite the banning of his film by the National Socialists in Germany, and in

April 1931 his novel *Der Weg Zurück* (*The Road Back*) was published. This did little to improve his popularity with the German authorities as it charted the slow recovery of traumatised soldiers following the war. Sensing growing unrest in his home country, Remarque purchased a villa in Switzerland on Lake Maggiore. In common with many authors, Remarque became a victim of the German authorities who took steps to discredit him - suggesting that he was really of Jewish descent and that his name was really Kramer (Remark spelled backwards), although there is absolutely no evidence of any truth in this allegation. He was also charged, prosecuted and fined for illegally removing money from Germany. As a final insult, his books, along with thousands of others, were publicly burned in Berlin.

As the Second World War approached, rumours reached Remarque that Ilsa, who had joined him at his villa, may lose her Swiss visa and be forced to return to Germany. In 1938, Remarque remarried her to save her from this fate. They agreed, however, that theirs would be an 'open' marriage and both were now exiled from Germany. In March 1939, they travelled to America, where Remarque would remain for the next nine years. During this time, he became involved in film making and script writing and had affairs with Marlene Dietrich and Greta Garbo. He also worked to help other immigrants, who were without sufficient funds to support themselves.

In December 1943, Remarque's youngest sister, Elfriede, was sentenced to death in Germany for 'undermining military forces'. She was beheaded. His stepmother, Maria, committed suicide shortly after the end of the Second World War, although Remarque himself did not return to Europe until 1948, when in May, he met up with his father in Switzerland.

In May 1951, Remarque began seeing the actress Paulette Goddard. The following year, after over a decade away, Remarque returned briefly to Osnabrück. He did not return again until two years later, when he attended his father's funeral. The formality of a divorce from Ilsa took place in 1957 and the following year, he married Paulette Goddard. They lived together until his death in Locarno, Switzerland on 25th September 1970. Paulette Goddard, who survived her husband by twenty years, is buried in the same cemetery as him in Switzerland.

Further Reading Recommendations for Students

Students are often expected to demonstrate a sound knowledge of the texts which they are studying and also to enhance this knowledge with extensive reading of other books within this genre. I have provided on the following pages a list of books, poetry, plays and non-fiction which, in my opinion, provide a good basic understanding of this topic. In addition, a small review of each book has been provided to help students choose which of the following are most suitable for them.

NOVELS

STRANGE MEETING by Susan Hill

Strange Meeting is a beautiful and moving book. It is the story of two young men, who meet in the worst circumstances, yet manage to overcome their surroundings and form a deep and lasting friendship. They are opposites: John Hilliard is quiet and reserved, while David Barton is outgoing and friendly. Despite their differences, their friendship blossoms, as the world around them disintegrates into self-destruction. Susan Hill writes so evocatively that the reader is automatically drawn into the lives of these men: the sights, sounds and even smells which they witness are brought to life. This is a book about war and its effects; it is also a story of love, both conventional and 'forbidden'; of human relationships of every variety. This is a tale told during the worst of times, about the best of men and is, quite simply, one of the best novels ever written about the First World War.

BIRDSONG by Sebastian Faulks

Written in 1993, this novel tells the story of Stephen Wraysford, his destructive pre-war love-affair, his war experiences and, through the eyes of his granddaughter, the effects of the war on his personality and his generation. A central theme to this story is man's ability to overcome adversity: to rise above his circumstances and survive - no matter what is thrown in his path. Many readers find the first part of this novel difficult to get through, but it is worth persevering. The pre-war section of the novel is essential in the understanding of Stephen Wraysford's character and his reactions to the events which happen later. Faulks's descriptions of battle scenes are among the best in this genre. In our view, this novel is suitable only for A-Level students, due to some adult themes.

A VERY LONG ENGAGEMENT by Sebastien Japrisot

A story of enduring love, truth and determination. Refusing to believe that her fiancé can possibly have left her forever, Mathilde decides to search for Manech whom she has been told is missing, presumed dead. She learns from a first-hand witness, that he may not have died, so she sets out on a voyage of discovery - learning not just about his fate, but also a great deal about herself and human nature. Mathilde herself has to overcome her own personal fears and hardships and, out of sheer persistence and a refusal to accept the obvious, she eventually discovers the truth. Although this novel does not form part of the main syllabus reading list, it does make an interesting and fairly easy read and is useful from the perspective that it gives a French woman's viewpoint of the war.

REGENERATION by Pat Barker

This book is, as its title implies, a novel about the rebuilding of men following extreme trauma. Billy Prior is a young working-class officer - a 'temporary gentleman' - who finds himself at Craiglockhart Military Hospital in Edinburgh, having been damaged by his experiences on the Western Front. It is the job of Dr W. H. R. Rivers, to 'mend' Prior, and others like him, ready for them to return to the fighting, while wrestling with his own conscience at the same time. Interweaved into this central plot is the meeting, also at Craiglockhart, of poets Siegfried Sassoon and Wilfred Owen, who are both there to receive treatment. This mixture of fact and fiction within a novel has created some controversy, but it is a common feature within this genre and one which Pat Barker handles better than most. This is an immensely useful book - even if not read as part of the Trilogy - as it takes place away from the front lines, showing the reader the deep and long-lasting effects of battle upon men, whose lives would never be the same again. Due to some adult content, we recommend this book for A-Level students only.

THE RETURN OF THE SOLDIER by Rebecca West

Written in 1918, this home-front novel gives a useful insight into the trauma of war, as seen through the eyes of three women. Chris Baldry, an officer and husband of Kitty, returns home suffering from shell-shock and amnesia, believing that he is still in a relationship with Margaret Allington - his first love. Kitty, Margaret and Chris's cousin, Jenny, must decide whether to leave Chris in his make-believe world, safe from the war; or whether to 'cure' him and risk his future welfare once he returns to being a soldier.

A LONG LONG WAY by Sebastian Barry

Sebastian Barry's novel tells the a story of Willie Dunne, a young Irish volunteer serving in the trenches of the Western Front. Willie must not only contend with the horrors of the war, but also his own confused feelings regarding the Easter uprising of 1916, and his father's disapproval. Willie's feelings and doubts lead to great upheavals in his life, including personal losses and betrayals by those whom he had believed he could trust. This is an interesting novel about loyalty, war and love, although it does suffer from a degree of historical inaccuracy. In our opinion, due to the adult content of this novel, it is suitable only for A-Level students.

NOT SO QUIET... by Helen Zenna Smith

This novel describes the lives of women working very close to the front line on the Western Front during the First World War, as ambulance drivers. Theirs is a dangerous job, in harsh conditions, with little or no respite. Helen (or Smithy, as she is called by her friends), eventually breaks down under the pressure of the work and returns, briefly, to England. An excellent novel for studying the female perspective, as well as the home front.

POETRY

It is recommended that students read from a wide variety of poets, including female writers. The following anthologies provide good resources for students.

POEMS OF THE FIRST WORLD WAR - NEVER SUCH INNOCENCE
Edited by Martin Stephen

Probably one of the finest anthologies of First World War poetry currently available. Martin Stephen has collected together some of the best known works by some of the most famous and well-read poets and mixed these with more obscure verses, including many by women and those on the home-front, together with some popular songs both from home and from the front. These have been interspersed with excellent notes which give the reader sufficient information without being too weighty. At the back of the book, there are short biographical notes on many of the poets. This is a fine anthology, suitable both for those who are starting out with their studies, and for the more experienced reader.

LADS: LOVE POETRY OF THE TRENCHES by Martin Taylor

Featuring many lesser-known poets and poems, this anthology approaches the First World War from a different perspective: love. A valuable introduction discusses the emotions of men who, perhaps for the first time, were discovering their own capacity to love their fellow man. This is not an anthology of purely homo-erotic poems, but also features verses by those who had found affection and deep, lasting friendship in the trenches of the First World War.

SCARS UPON MY HEART
Selected by Catherine Reilly

First published in 1981, this anthology is invaluable as it features a collection of poems written exclusively by women on the subject of the First World War. Some of the better known female poets are featured here, such as Vera Brittain and Jessie Pope, but there are also many more writers who are less famous. In addition there are some poets whose work is featured, who are not now renowned for their poetry, but for their works in other areas of literature. Many of the poets included here have minor biographical details featured at the end of the anthology. This book has become the 'standard' for those wishing to study the female contribution to this genre.

UP THE LINE TO DEATH
Edited by Brian Gardner

This anthology, described by its editor Brian Gardner as a 'book about war', is probably, and deservedly, one of the most widely read in this genre. The famous and not-so-famous sit happily together within in these pages of carefully selected poetry. Arranged thematically, these poems provide a poet's-eye-view of the progression of the war, from the initial euphoria and nationalistic pride of John Freeman's 'Happy is England Now' to Sassoon's plea that we should 'never forget'. Useful biographical details and introductions complete this book, which is almost certainly the most useful and important of all the First World War poetry anthologies.

NON-FICTION

UNDERTONES OF WAR by Edmund Blunden

Edmund Blunden's memoir of his experiences in the First World War is a moving, enlightening and occasionally humorous book, demonstrating above all the intense feelings of respect and comradeship which Blunden found in the trenches.

MEMOIRS OF AN INFANTRY OFFICER by Siegfried Sassoon

Following on from *Memoirs of a Fox-hunting Man*, this book is an autobiographical account of Sassoon's life during the First World War. Sassoon has changed the names of the characters and George Sherston (Sassoon) is not a poet. Sassoon became one of the war's most famous poets and this prose account of his war provides useful background information.
(For a list of the fictional characters and their factual counterparts, see Appendix II of *Siegfried Sassoon* by John Stuart Roberts.)

THE GREAT WAR GENERALS ON THE WESTERN FRONT 1914-1918 by Robin Neillands

Like many others before and since, the cover of this book claims that it will dismiss the old myth that the troops who served in the First World War were badly served by their senior officers. Unlike most of the other books, however, this one is balanced and thought-provoking. Of particular interest within this book is the final chapter which provides an assessment of the main protagonists and their role in the conflict.

THE WESTERN FRONT by Richard Holmes

This is one of many history books about the First World War. Dealing specifically with the Western Front, Richard Holmes looks at the creation of the trench warfare system, supplying men and munitions, major battles and living on the front line.

LETTERS FROM A LOST GENERATION (FIRST WORLD WAR LETTERS OF VERA BRITTAIN AND FOUR FRIENDS)
Edited by Alan Bishop and Mark Bostridge

A remarkable insight into the changes which the First World War caused to a particular set of individuals. In this instance, Vera Brittain lost four important people in her life (two close friends, her fiancé and her brother). The agony this evoked is demonstrated through letters sent between these five characters, which went on to form the basis of Vera Brittain's autobiography *Testament of Youth*.

1914-1918: VOICES AND IMAGES OF THE GREAT WAR
by Lyn MacDonald

One of the most useful 'unofficial' history books available to those studying the First World War. This book tells the story of the soldiers who fought the war through their letters, diary extracts, newspaper reports, poetry and eye-witness accounts. As with all of Lyn MacDonald's excellent books, *Voices and Images of the Great War* tells its story through the words of the people who were there. The author gives just the right amount of background information of a political and historical nature to keep the reader interested and informed, while leaving the centre-stage to those who really matter... the men themselves.

GREAT WAR LITERATURE NOTES

BIBLIOGRAPHY

SIEGFRIED SASSOON - THE WAR POEMS Edited by Rupert Hart-Davis

SCARS UPON MY HEART Edited by Catherine Reilly

THE FIRST WORLD WAR by John Keegan

REGENERATION by Pat Barker

BIRDSONG by Sebastian Faulks

JOURNEY'S END by R. C. Sherriff

STRANGE MEETING by Susan Hill

THE RETURN OF THE SOLDIER by Rebecca West

POEMS OF THE FIRST WORLD WAR - NEVER SUCH INNOCENCE
Edited by Martin Stephen

WILFRED OWEN - WAR POEMS AND OTHERS Edited by Dominic Hibberd

GREAT WAR LITERATURE STUDY GUIDE TITLES

GREAT WAR LITERATURE STUDY GUIDE E-BOOKS:

NOVELS & PLAYS

All Quiet on the Western Front
Birdsong
Journey's End (A-Level or GCSE)
Regeneration
The Eye in the Door
The Ghost Road
A Long Long Way
The First Casualty
Strange Meeting
The Return of the Soldier
The Accrington Pals
Not About Heroes
Oh What a Lovely War

POET BIOGRAPHIES AND POETRY ANALYSIS:

Herbert Asquith
Harold Begbie
John Peale Bishop
Edmund Blunden
Vera Brittain
Rupert Brooke
Thomas Burke
May Wedderburn Cannan

Margaret Postgate Cole
Alice Corbin
E E Cummings
Nancy Cunard
T S Eliot
Eleanor Farjeon
Gilbert Frankau
Robert Frost
Wilfrid Wilson Gibson
Anna Gordon Keown
Robert Graves
Julian Grenfell
Ivor Gurney
Thomas Hardy
Alan P Herbert
Agnes Grozier Herbertson
W N Hodgson
A E Housman
Geoffrey Anketell Studdert Kennedy
Winifred M Letts
Amy Lowell
E A Mackintosh
John McCrae
Charlotte Mew
Edna St Vincent Millay
Ruth Comfort Mitchell
Harriet Monroe
Edith Nesbit
Robert Nichols
Wilfred Owen
Jessie Pope
Ezra Pound
Florence Ripley Mastin
Isaac Rosenberg
Carl Sandburg
Siegfried Sassoon
Alan Seeger
Charles Hamilton Sorley
Wallace Stevens
Sara Teasdale

Edward Wyndham Tennant
Lesbia Thanet
Edward Thomas
Iris Tree
Katharine Tynan Hinkson
Robert Ernest Vernède
Arthur Graeme West

Please note that e-books are only available direct from our Web site at www.greatwarliterature.co.uk and cannot be purchased through bookshops.

NOTES

NOTES

NOTES

www.ingramcontent.com/pod-product-compliance
Lightning Source LLC
Chambersburg PA
CBHW070058100426
42743CB00012B/2586